Smashing
Silos

Smashing Silos

The Accunomics Guide
to the New Normal

BOB SHAW

*accu*nomics

THE SCIENCE OF PROFITABILITY

NEW YORK | SINGAPORE

To my late father, Matthew J. Shaw, who often told me, "more often than not, people are exactly as they seem to be."

Bob Shaw

Going to work for a big company is like getting on a train. Are you going sixty miles an hour? Or is the train going sixty miles an hour and you're just sitting still?

J. Paul Getty

Contents

Preface

Like you, my bookshelves are packed with well-intentioned business books that failed to capture more than a cursory level of my attention. Why? Either they were written to convey complex theories that I couldn't imagine applying in practice, or they were case-study laden knock-offs of *In Search of Excellence* that couldn't come close to the impact of the original. I hope you'll find *Smashing Silos* to be different.

To begin, *Smashing Silos* is a novel. Writing a novel afforded me the opportunity to integrate all the important concepts that I wanted to convey into an easy-to-read format—a story that you'll hopefully want to read right through to its happy ending. Just as importantly, as is the case with any management consultant, I'm not at liberty to disclose my client's data, nor discuss their business issues or financial performance. Composing a work of fiction allowed me to roll many of the common issues I've experienced throughout my career into a single narrative, and manufacture all the charts and analysis necessary to illustrate my methodology. Since my process deals with a corporation's most detailed and sensitive profitability data, developing a rich fictional database was really the only plausible option.

However, while the business, characters and data in *Smashing Silos* are fictional, the issues presented and the approaches to solving them are very real. With the help of my colleagues at Accunomics, we reviewed dozens of engagements, and identified the common challenges that effect many businesses. We ensured that every chart and financial scenario in the book represented real findings from real projects, even though the numbers are disguised. Likewise, the characters are composites of the personality traits that I've encountered throughout my career, with perhaps just a little additional color to make the story as enjoyable as possible.

If the story keeps you engaged to the end, I've accomplished my first objective. My second objective is to share a practical methodology for transforming the profitability of a business. It's a methodology that I've developed over the years with the help of my colleagues and clients, and it has proven effective in driving 300+ percent earnings improvements in my clients' businesses. But don't confuse "practical" with "easy." At the heart of *Smashing Silos* are two extremely challenging issues: overcoming corporate inertia and politics, and gleaning actionable insights from corporate financial data. Both obstacles can only be tackled with an extraordinary level of perseverance and hard work—plus some technically savvy analysis. In most cases, you'll even need to bring in some outside help.

In my thirty years of consulting to some of the world's largest corporations, I've consistently found that the biggest impediment to turning around a business is underestimating the organization's inertia to change. Corporations naturally evolve into silos—by division, function, department, and even by team. Each silo has its own objectives, whether officially set by the manager or de facto adopted by its members. These silos become an albatross for change agents, as their members cling to their objectives and their methods despite the needs of the business. The silos are often protected by their leaders, both for personal status and to avoid the inevitable pain of change. In many cases, the complexity of the corporation makes it too hard for people to think outside their silo; they instead choose to focus on what they know and can control. Breaking down these silos and orienting employees toward the business' bottom line is imperative to achieving a breakthrough level of profitability.

When Jim Collins tells us that "good is the enemy of great" in his book *Good to Great*, he seems to concentrate mostly on capability or heritage as the keys to greatness. In my experience, capability is overrated. Most companies are capable of being great, but are unable to overcome their own inertia to become great. A major contributor to this problem is "Corporate Speak." While intended to inspire sensitivity and promote the free exchange of ideas, corporate cultures and communications norms often mask the true deficiencies in a business. In this type of environment, with a lack of internal challenges and leadership's natural aversion to tough decisions, silos endure, and greatness remains elusive.

Overcoming inertia and breaking down silos need not be confrontational, but it almost always needs to be critical and factual. Over the years, I've found that the best way to battle the silos and get an organization moving forward is with a mountain of data. Profitability metrics, such as net operating income or return on capital, are the most impactful. It's simply tough to argue that change is needed when you're losing money, even if your other operating metrics look great. At Accunomics, we use profitability data as the key element of our change process, and that's why I place such a heavy emphasis on data and data analysis in *Smashing Silos*.

Following years of massive investments in enterprise IT applications— enterprise resource planning, customer relationship management and business intelligence, to name a few—most corporations are awash in data. While it's extremely rare to hear executives and employees complain about too much useful information, they certainly do complain about too much data, not enough analysis, and not enough meaningful insight. Surprisingly, fully-loaded profitability data is the toughest to find or develop, even though it's the most meaningful to the business' success. In fairness, most corporations have high quality financial statements at the business unit level, and some form of sales and margin reporting down to the territory level. However, few can identify bottom line profitability by customer, product, or sales rep, much less by individual "ship-to" location or order. Yet, this is exactly the level of information that most frontline employees and supervisors need to impact profitability.

Admittedly, measuring profitability down to these granular levels is my passion. I believe in a simple premise: if you can make even the smallest improvements to the most important drivers of profitability all at the same time, the net impact on earnings can be dramatic. This is typically what separates good performance from great performance. But to get at these high impact changes, you must have extremely rigorous data preparation, dissemination, and review processes, and achieve a level of precision in your reporting that goes well beyond the standard divisional income statement. Without such precision, your ability to get at the true root causes of your business issues and make the surgical adjustments I advocate will be limited. You won't have the mountain of data you need to smash the silos, and you'll be stuck at "good" or worse performance.

Analyzing and transforming a multi-hundred million-dollar business unit is a massive undertaking. The scope of *Smashing Silos* only allows for a fraction of the necessary analysis to be presented and discussed. Nonetheless, my colleagues and I want readers to have access to a more comprehensive sampling of the analysis underlying the story. To accomplish this goal, our team has constructed a companion website for *Smashing Silos* at www.smashing-silos.com that contains over eighty slides of analysis, profiles and biographies. We've designed the site as a virtual "war room," enabling the reader to go online to see and hear the character's complete presentations as they occur in the story. Any time you see the graphic below in the text, I encourage you to visit the war room to dig deeper into the process:

VIRTUAL WAR ROOM — Review Briefings, Bios and Presentations On-Line at www.smashing-silos.com

In closing, let me say thank you for embarking on this read. Please enjoy it, and always remember that any corporation has the potential to become great—it starts with you.

Bob Shaw
Far Hills, New Jersey

Chapter 1

Scratch The Surface

"Do you have a minute?" Linda Thomas felt a tap on her shoulder as she walked out of the conference room at the end of the Monday executive team meeting. She spun around. It was Elliot Davis, her executive vice president.

"Of course."

"We're having a dinner tonight for George to mark his retirement from Surgitec. It's late notice, I know. But it'd be great if you could make it. Lots of the old team will be there."

"He's retiring already? I thought he had still had a couple of months. What time?"

"Six-thirty drinks, seven-fifteen dinner. It's at the Main Line Club. Shouldn't take you more than fifteen minutes to get there."

"Speeches?"

"Probably, but nothing you'll need to prepare. Just an old-fashioned send-off for one of our own…very casual. George will probably want us all singing Irish songs around the piano by the end."

"Let me check. But I'm pretty sure I can be there."

"Great. It'd be great for morale. With George going, everyone over at Surgitec is feeling a little uneasy. A visit from the boss would do them a world of good."

Linda nodded. Her mind was still half on the meeting that had just passed. She had been disturbed by the lack of urgency within her senior team. "We haven't decided on a replacement yet for George, have we?"

"Don't worry about it," said Elliot. "I've got a guy lined up. He's worked with

BUSINESS OVERVIEW   Review Surgitec's Business Overview On-Line at www.smashing-silos.com

me for years. Trustworthy. Dependable. He won't rock the boat. He'll just keep pulling out the cash. Thought I'd take that off your plate, given everything else you're dealing with."

"Fine, fine," said Linda, keen to escape Elliot. But as she walked toward her office, she felt uneasy. It had been just six months since she had won the CEO job, beating out Elliot and one other candidate. She had toured the company, introduced herself, studied every business unit and geography in detail, and committed herself to make changes. But with every step she took, she felt dragged down into the quicksand of this place, the complacency, the comfort, the well-padded inertia. It was a daily battle to stay ahead, to stay light and nimble, ready for anything.

"Won't rock the boat," Elliot had said. The thing was, Linda reflected, the company badly needed boat-rockers. Not exactly pirates and buccaneers, but at least men and women ready to challenge the status quo and imagine a better future. Otherwise, what were they all doing there? Filling out HR questionnaires and waiting like George for retirement—for the gold watch, the final "attaboy" and the slow shuffle toward a condo in Florida?

Linda turned into her office and closed the door. She had barely had time to furnish it. The walls still showed the outline of the last CEO's art collection. Linda's predecessor had plastered the walls with signed artwork by Chagall and Miro. Linda had a few pictures of her own, but they were gathering dust in her attic at home. She had every intention of making this office her own, but through her impact on the organization, not through its décor.

When she had taken the job, Linda had requested a performance-based contract—a compensation package that rewarded her in line with shareholders. She didn't want to go down the path of other Fortune 100 chief executives and hire decorators for her private office, lavishing company money on $1,000 wastebaskets and $40,000 rugs. She wanted the company to know that she was as cost-focused as anyone else. From now on, she wanted the company to know that performance and performance alone was what mattered. The fact that she was the first woman to run Carson was an issue for the media to fuss about. Here inside the company, there was work to be done.

She pressed the buzzer on her desk.

"Can I have the latest file on Surgitec please, Ellen?"

Two minutes later, her assistant bustled in holding a manila file. Ellen had risen through the ranks with Linda. She was ten years older than her and shared many of her traits. She deplored waste, whether of money or time. She was efficient but never rude. And she adored the company she worked for. Linda had made sure she received stock options over the years, which had enabled her to buy a more than decent home and send three daughters through private college. For that alone, she was ferociously loyal.

"Thanks," said Linda, as she opened the file. On top was the press release announcing George's retirement. Forty years at Carson Corporation, fifteen of which he had spent running Surgitec. There were quotes from hospital bosses and head surgeons, chiefs of HMOs and state health care officials, all regretting George's imminent departure—"a legend," "the most loved man in healthcare," "a friend first, a business partner second," "never a dull moment with George around."

There was an 8" x 10" glossy showing George in his office, looking every inch the prototypical businessman —his grey hair slicked back, his teeth and wing-tips shining, a razor-sharp press in the pants of his pinstripe suit. He was standing beside his desk, leaning on a putter. There was a photograph in a silver frame turned so anyone sitting across the table from George could see it. It showed him on the Old Course at St. Andrews in Scotland, his arm thrown around the golf legend Tom Watson. As George never failed to tell you, Watson was one of his oldest friends.

George's story was well known throughout Carson. He had made his name as a pharmaceutical salesman, starting out in the rural areas of West Virginia, before proving himself worthy of the big accounts, the hospitals and chains of doctors' practices. He had then joined the executive ranks, quickly rising to the top job at Surgitec, which sold supplies to hospitals and clinics—trays, syringes, scrubs, pretty much anything doctors might need except drugs or serious electrical equipment. It had been a perfect fit. George was the ultimate glad-hander, and Surgitec was the ultimate foundation business for Carson: a low-growth but a bulletproof source of free cash flow. All George had to do was not screw it up. And he had succeeded brilliantly.

The employees at Surgitec adored him. As he walked the corridors of the head office, he had a word for everyone, from the head of manufacturing to the night janitor. His annual golf tournament for the sales force was a raucous affair that rotated around the best courses of Arizona, Nevada, and Southern California. But the salesmen's families loved him too, for his courtesy and interest at company outings, and the bonuses he gave them every December.

Customers liked George because they could always pick up the phone and talk to him. He was always there to smooth over any problem, to trim a price here and there, or make sure a delivery arrived tomorrow rather than Monday. Nothing was ever too much for George. And then of course he was just so damned funny. There wasn't a dirty story or scurrilous yarn he didn't know, and wasn't ready to deliver down the phone in his stagey whisper. Even Linda had to smile as she thought of the love George elicited inside and outside the company.

Next were the latest financial results, headed by a graph showing steady performance and growth over the past five years. There was nothing spectacular about Surgitec. But if, like Linda, you were running a company with $12 billion in annual sales, Surgitec offered the reassurance of offering nothing to worry about. As she shuffled through the financials, Linda found Surgitec's balance sheet. She glanced at its assets. She flicked back to the latest annual income statement. She reached forward to pick up a pencil from her desk. She scribbled a few numbers down on a notepad—profit before interest and tax...divide it by capital employed. She tried the calculation in her head. No, surely that was wrong.

She reached for the old pocket calculator she kept in a lower desk drawer. It confirmed her mental calculation. Carson expected its businesses to produce a return on capital employed of 20 percent, yet Surgitec was down at 4.5 percent. A $1.2 billion business underperforming and no one seemed to care.

She buzzed again. "Ellen, could you pull the last five years of Surgitec's financials?" A few minutes later, Ellen arrived with a thicker file.

"Anything I can help you with?" she asked.

"No thanks," said Linda distractedly, as she opened up the file. She started with the year before last then kept going back, scribbling on the pad.

(Millions $)	2006	2007	2008	2009	2010
Sales	1,033.8	1,080.9	1,137.5	1,177.6	1,205.9
Cost of Goods Sold	560.3	570.7	607.4	607.6	597.0
Gross Profit	473.5	510.2	530.1	570.0	608.9
Research & Development	78.6	78.9	93.3	93.0	104.0
Selling , General & Admin	320.5	352.4	384.5	429.8	460.6
Operating Expenses	399.0	431.3	477.8	522.9	564.6
Operating Income	74.4	78.9	52.3	47.1	44.3
Income Taxes	25.7	26.7	17.9	16.6	15.4
Net Income	48.8	52.2	34.4	30.5	28.9
Invested Capital	997.3	992.4	894.4	989.6	984.5
Return on Capital %	7.4%	7.9%	5.8%	4.8%	4.5%
Net Margin %	4.7%	4.8%	3.0%	2.6%	2.4%

Year after year, Surgitec had been reporting rising sales, but its ROCE was stuck in the low single digits. It was the story of Carson in a microcosm. On the surface, it was a champion of corporate America, a thoroughly good citizen. Like the expensive brand advertising authorized by Linda's predecessor said, Carson was about "Wellness for the World."

But scratch below the surface and you found a company on auto-pilot, protected by deep moats of market share, a stable of predictable products, and broad industry influence. Industry forces kept Carson afloat. All that its generations of captains and passengers had to do was make sure the supertanker didn't sink. Do that, and they were guaranteed jobs and pensions for life.

Linda flipped the file shut and leaned back in her chair. The sun was setting now over the oak trees that dotted the corporate campus. A shaft of red light pierced the towering iron sculpture placed in the center of the main garden outside her office. It was a twentieth century masterpiece, she had been told. She tapped the edge of the table with her pencil and thought back to how she had gotten this job.

Elliot had joined Carson three years before her. For years, many people had considered him a shoo-in for the top job. But a botched acquisition five years earlier had allowed Linda to cut past him on the executive ladder.

Elliot had been convinced by a group of Wall Street bankers that Carson had to deploy some of its cash reserves, and the best way was to buy a smaller, though seemingly more strategic, competitor. The synergies, they told him, would lead to growth. He had believed them and invested his entire reputation in the deal. He hoped it would be the decisive pass, the bullet downfield that would bring his career galloping into the end zone.

The banks made a fortune in fees for advising Carson and structuring debt for the deal, while their proprietary trading desks made a killing arbitraging the merger. The then CEO had reveled in the attention it brought him, the *BusinessWeek* cover showing him standing with his arms folded, staring forbiddingly into the camera's lens, the lunch with the *Financial Times*, and the ten-minute spot with Maria Bartiromo, the Money Honey, on CNBC. It brought a welcome dash of spice to the otherwise bland corporate diet of earnings, analyst calls, strategic reviews, and plant visits.

A couple of the board members had objected. "Seventy percent of mergers fail," they kept saying. "Don't let the money burn a hole in the company's pocket. If you don't like holding it, why not return it to shareholders?" But Elliot and the CEO were now set on their path. The bankers had given them a taste of what it meant to be Wall Street players, and they were hooked. They had pushed them into the media glare and now the CEO did not want to be seen as a chicken. He wanted more lunches at San Pietro, a few tables away from Jack Welch. He could suddenly see his post-Carson life stretching away, a catalog of glittering board memberships in New York and around the world. It promised so much more than being head of the President's Circle at the Philadelphia Symphony Orchestra.

But then all of the synergies that seemed so easy became nearly impossible to achieve. Within two years, it became obvious that Carson had paid about 40 percent more than it should have; the bankers had ripped them off. But rather than ever admitting as much, the company did what big companies often do. It announced that the CEO would be retiring as planned within a couple of years and that the search would begin for his successor. The rest of those involved would carry on, only mildly chastened.

Despite being so closely linked to the merger, Elliot was still among the favored candidates to be the next CEO. On paper, he had all the required experience. He had worked in various functions, and had run a major territory, Latin America, albeit from the comfort of Miami. He had overseen large P&Ls, but perhaps most important of all, he had nuzzled up close to certain members of the board. Everyone in the company knew it, and it gave him power, especially among his peers. It was a weapon he rarely used, but at certain key moments in his career, Elliot had used his boardroom relationships to influence vital decisions.

The CEO selection process had gone on for months. Linda, Elliot, and the third candidate, Bruce Jardine, had had their P&Ls picked over. They had been invited to present to the board, institutional investors, and overseas partners. Their spouses had been vetted, their peers and subordinates interviewed. An expensive recruiting firm had overseen the process. Going into the final week, Elliot was confident of success and close observers in the office noticed a strut about him. But then came the article in *Barron's*.

Elliot's front-runner status had leaked out. Linda didn't put it past Elliot to have leaked it himself, in order to make his ascent seem a lock. If so, his tactic misfired. *Barron's* wrote that Elliot's association with the ill-fated merger should rule him out of succession. "Lots of large corporations go through challenging mergers," the newspaper's main columnist wrote, "but Carson does so more rarely than others. If it hopes to retain its well-earned reputation for caution, discipline, and sound stewardship, it would be foolish to reward an executive so closely identified with the least glorious chapter in its recent history with the keys to the kingdom."

When the decision had to be made, Linda squeaked in. Elliot's supporters on the board argued vociferously for him, but the *Barron's* piece had sowed too many doubts. After the vote, Elliot had knocked on Linda's door.

"Congratulations." Linda could see the tightness in his smile.

"It was a close decision. Thanks for a fair fight."

"If you need anything, I'm here for you, Linda, even after this. Carson has been my life and I hope we can work together in the future."

"I appreciate it, Elliot. I'm looking forward to it, too. I think we can achieve a lot."

"I know you had nothing to do with the *Barron's* piece." Linda was stunned.

It had never even crossed her mind that Elliot might suspect her of leaking a story to the press. It had never been her style. "I don't know if it was decisive, but just so you know. I don't blame you for it."

Linda pushed a newspaper round her desk with her index finger. She didn't know what to say. Elliot filled the silence.

"You've probably got a lot on your plate. I'll see you later."

The telephone rang, jolting Linda from her recollections.

"What time will you be home tonight?"

"Around nine, I guess," she said to her husband.

"So you'll be missing Adam's hockey game."

"Yes…yes," she stammered. "How many more does he have this season?"

"One, Linda, after this one. You've missed all eight so far."

"I know. Say sorry to him, will you? Tonight's important. A retirement party. I have to put in an appearance. You know how it is."

"At least I don't have to come, I guess."

"Count your blessings."

She set the phone back in its cradle. What could she do about Surgitec? If she let Elliot manage the succession, it would be an admission of defeat. An admission that the old routines still apply. That she was just another warm body occupying the finest suite of offices in the building. But she couldn't just say no. She had to have an alternative.

She stepped to the window. The thick glass meant that no noise penetrated her office from the outside. In the distance, she could see her employees start to trickle out of the main entrance toward their cars. She checked her watch. 5 p.m. on the dot.

Out of the corner of her eye, she saw a copy of the latest company newsletter. It was a glossy thing, which came out every month at considerable expense. On the cover was a photograph of a climbing frame in a playground in Paris. There was the mayor, a wizened old Frenchman, and next to him the head of Carson - France, David Hewitt.

Linda picked it up and took a closer look. Hewitt had worked for her years ago. They hadn't seen each other in a while, but Linda had always followed his career from a distance. He was in many ways the perfect Carson man—hard-working, modest, intelligent, ready to do whatever he was asked, but also with a vein of dark humor buried beneath his pleasant Midwestern exterior. Linda had always liked him personally and admired his work.

She stepped back to her desk, and brought up Hewitt's page in the corporate directory: forty-three years old, married, two children, head of France for the past eighteen months, and based in Paris. He had joined Carson straight out of the University of Notre Dame, spent two years on the rotational program, then moved around from manufacturing to sales and then finance, learning the ropes. Linda tried accessing Hewitt's HR records, but the files were locked.

"Ellen," she buzzed. "How do I get into these HR files?"

She came in and with a few keystrokes and unlocked them. Hewitt's scores were impeccable. In every position he had held, he had excelled. But now he was in the holding pattern familiar to so many executives at Carson. They hit their mid-forties, and suddenly they faced the sharp narrowing of the pyramid. These were the years when many of them analyzed the odds of reaching the top and decided they would do better elsewhere. And there were always plenty of other companies willing to hire Carson executives, given the thorough training they had received.

"What time is it in Paris?" she asked Ellen through the open door to her office.

"Six hours ahead. So eleven p.m."

"Too late to call then. On a Friday night? At home?"

"Yes."

"You sure? I mean most are just finishing dinner."

"Don't be one of those bosses, Linda. Leave the poor man alone. Unless it's absolutely urgent." Linda hesitated before dialing the home number listed for Hewitt. It rang several times before clicking over to an answering machine. "You've reached the Hewitt family. Please leave a message. Merci!"

Linda was a little flustered, but decided to press on. Having made the call, she didn't want Hewitt seeing the number on his phone and wondering why the CEO was crank calling him at eleven o'clock on a Friday night.

"David, it's Linda Thomas here. Sorry to be calling you so late. But I wanted to ask if you could fly back to Philadelphia early next week to talk. It's about Surgitec. I'd like to put your name in the hat. If you are interested, we'd like to move quickly. So if you could be here early next week, that would be great. Have a great weekend, and do send my best to your family."

Linda picked her light, gray jacket from the back of her chair and slipped it over her shoulders. She was ready now for the send-off for George. Casual, Elliot had said. A few words of thanks, a joke about his golf game, stay for dinner. Out with the old.

And provided Hewitt came through, in with the new.

Chapter 2

Out With The Old

Linda's car passed along the swooping driveway to the Main Line Country Club, past the first and tenth holes of the golf course. She could see only two carts whizzing around the empty fairways, but the parking lot in front of the grand, 1890s clubhouse was packed. Men in suits and women in cocktail dresses were stepping out of expensive cars and crunching across the gravel to the entrance. She saw Elliot standing by the main door greeting them as they arrived. He was in a suit and tie as well. Why had he said it was casual? As Linda's car turned into the lot, she felt suddenly under-dressed for the occasion. It was too late for her to go back. Elliot had already spied her.

Linda stepped out the car. A photographer from the company magazine snapped her arrival. Elliot walked up and shook her by the hand.

"Thanks so much, Linda. It'll mean so much to George."

"It's the least I could do."

Elliot accompanied her through the door into the soaring, oak paneled lobby. Waiters and waitresses flitted among the guests, carrying trays loaded with drinks. A six-piece jazz band played in a corner, filling the room with their cheerful music. And in the midst of it all was George, greeting everyone as if he were running for president, smiling, slapping backs, and whispering in ears.

"These aren't all company people," Linda murmured to Elliot.

"No. A lot are Surgitec customers and old friends of George."

"Personal friends?"

"You know there's no difference between personal and business for an old sales hand like George."

A waitress approached Linda. She took a glass of white wine, thanked her, and stepped toward the crowd. George saw her and pressed through the waves of well-wishers, like a mighty ship pressing through a churning sea. He reached out to shake Linda's hand. George's leathery hand enveloped Linda's. He also placed a hand on Linda's shoulder, to the point where Linda felt she was being pulled in by a force field of charm.

"So glad you could make it, Linda," he said, beaming. "Really great of you to come. Let me introduce you around." The next fifteen minutes were a blur of men and women in evening dress, customers large and small, distributors, salesmen, and secretaries from Surgitec, all fans of George.

Dinner was served in a cavernous dining room, more appropriate for an English king than a corporate send-off. But then the grandees of Philadelphia had always had an elevated sense of their importance.

Linda checked her watch. It was already 7:40 and dinner had not yet begun. She could see the wait-staff hovering. Elliot sat on the other side of Linda's table, between the wives of another Carson executive and the head of a major HMO.

Adam would be on the rink now, getting toward the end of the first period. Ten years earlier, Linda would take him to early morning practices on the ice and drive him to his first games. She loved the bracing cold of the rinks, stamping her feet and warming her hands with plastic cups of bad coffee, talking to the other parents and watching her young son surge uncertainly across the ice, groping for the puck. Now Adam was a star, a six-foot-two-inch forward who flew dizzyingly around the rinks of Pennsylvania, New York, and New Jersey, amassing scoring titles and prep school championships at will. But now that Linda was chief executive, she was missing every moment of her son's achievements. While her husband was watching Adam, she was stuck here watching three hundred people chew and drink their way through a good portion of Carson's hard won wealth.

The starter was a stuffed lobster claw surrounded by a circle of vivid green oil. Linda prized out the contents with her fork. Everyone around her was drinking wine. The mood was raucous and merry. George leaned in to get the table's attention.

"Tomorrow morning, I'm flying out to Pebble Beach for eighteen holes with Tom Watson. I've known Tom for years and this is his retirement present—just got to make sure I don't shank my first drive into the Pacific Ocean." He lifted up his half-full wine glass and tapped it with the nail of his little finger. "This is not going to help." Everyone at the table roared with laughter.

Linda twisted her wedding ring around her finger, waiting for her moment to speak. It came eventually with the arrival of dessert, three wobbling brown lumps, which the chef had optimistically called a "chocolate medley." Elliot tapped his wine glass and the room fell quiet. He nodded at Linda, who pushed her chair back and rose to speak.

"There's an old saying that when you're hiring someone to run a business, the last thing you want to see is a low golf handicap." A nervous quiet filled the room. "George, I am happy to say, is the exception." George threw his head back and laughed and the other guests followed suit. "Surgitec and Carson will never be quite the same. He has enriched all of our lives professionally, but more importantly, personally. They say that people do business with people they like. Never has that seemed clearer to me than this evening. Many people in business leave behind nothing but a laundry list of targets met, quotas filled, and meetings attended. George has done all of that quite brilliantly. But far more important, he leaves behind days brightened, jokes shared, and friends made. It has been a remarkable ride. Today, with sadness as a CEO losing a valued colleague, but with joy as a friend watching a man head into a well-earned retirement, I ask you all to raise a glass to George. And to many nineteenth holes to come. To George." With the scraping of chairs and creaking of knees, everyone in the room rose. George looked over at Linda, put his hands together as if in prayer, and bowed his head in thanks.

"Great speech, Linda," said Elliot, catching her as he prepared to leave. "Short and sweet."

"Thanks Elliot. Looks like it will be a long night." The band had just started up again. The dance floor was packed. From the look of the awkward gyrations, there would be several pulled muscles and aching backs tomorrow morning.

"George deserves it. After all he's done."

"About George. Or rather about his successor."

"Yes, it's all in hand. Got just the guy."

"I'm sure you do. But for appearances' sake, if nothing else, I'd like to see a contest. So I've asked David Hewitt to come over from France next week for an interview."

"Hewitt? France? What does he know about hospital supplies?"

"Hewitt has an extremely balanced resume of accomplishments at Carson and I think you will be impressed when you take the time to review his credentials." Linda could see George had removed his jacket and was doing a lame version of "The Running Man" on the dance floor.

"Whatever you say, Linda. But I think you'll be impressed by the person I have lined up for this."

"I'm sure I will. In any case, have a great weekend. I'll see you on Monday."

Linda walked over to her car. Her driver opened the back door. She checked her watch again. 10:20 p.m. She had missed Adam's game completely. And by the time she got home, Adam would be locked in his room, lost in his computer. And her husband would be in bed, probably with the lights out. All so she could say a few words for a retiring executive, who, Linda realized after looking at the numbers, had done much more for himself than he had ever done for Carson's shareholders.

She flicked on the light in the back of the car and reached for the stack of papers Ellen had given her to read. They were organized with her usual precision, color coded by priority. She reached for one of the documents marked with a red label. A fight had broken out with one of the corporation's major distributors. The distributor wanted a larger piece of the action. Didn't they always? Another document gave a progress report on the construction of a new research center in India. Carson was a globe-spanning enterprise, with billions of dollars in sales and tens of thousands of employees. Surgitec was just a small piece of the business. But it was one of the earliest parts of Carson. Its headquarters was close to Carson's. Other business units might come and go, but Surgitec was family. Nonetheless, Linda was done with its "good ole boy" processes. If you allowed your cronies to run the business units, you were doomed. No one would take her seriously. Now George was gone, Surgitec would have to stand on its own feet and earn its place within Carson. There could be no excuses for protecting it anymore, no matter how many points Elliot felt that might win him with the board and the company's longest-standing employees. Surgitec's improvement was going to be vital to Linda's own credibility as an agent of change.

Three thousand miles away, David Hewitt stared up at his bedroom ceiling.

His mind was fuzzy from too much red wine and an ill-advised Cognac to round off dinner. And now this. Linda Thomas calling in person. Surgitec? Luckily he had got to the answering machine before his wife. She was just getting to like Paris. The last thing he wanted to tell her was to pack up and come back to Philadelphia. Rittenhouse Square was not a patch on the Rue Faubourg St. Honore, and the Liberty Bell was no Eiffel Tower.

What on earth was he going to do?

Chapter 3

So Much For That

Thwack!

The dimpled ball soared off the face of David's driver into the pale blue sky and landed 280 yards away in the middle of the fairway. A near perfect drive.

"I think I'm actually better when I'm a little hung over." He shook his head to clear the fog of the night before. Standing behind him were three of his oldest and closest friends. They had flown in from the United States with their wives for a short holiday in Paris.

"It's because you're more relaxed," said Marc, a dentist from New York City, who went to college with David. "Golf is all in the head. A few drinks the night before and you're not bothered by all your usual daily concerns when you get to the first tee." He took a practice swing and winced. His back still ached from the long flight two days before. "But still, that last bottle was probably not a good idea." He swung again and the ball sliced right toward the adjacent fairway.

"Come on guys! We're in Paris. The last bottle is always a good idea." Jim had joined Carson with David in the same graduate trainee program. Their careers had followed very similar paths until the past two years. While David had gone to France, Jim had taken charge of a new, high-potential biotech business unit. Carson was plowing capital into the young business unit, and Elliot Davis had championed the view that the corporation's future rested on this and similar ventures. Jim now travelled frequently to Silicon Valley and was a constant presence at biotech conferences. It was a bracing change from his years in the veterinary products unit, and marked him as a rising star. His set of clubs was far and away the most expensive in the foursome. He plucked out behemoth of a driver from his bag.

"This is the life, Hewitt. Paris. Golf next door to a chateau. I'd hang onto this gig as long as you can." He waggled his hips and lined up his shot. He swung hard and missed. The other three men doubled over laughing. Jim scowled, lined himself up again, and struck the ball, landing it thirty feet short of the green. "Go to hell, guys."

Last up was Jason. He had to borrow a pair of slacks from David. His bags had been lost en route. "You know, I never get to play this game," he said.

"I can tell," said Jim, as Jason took an awkward practice swing.

"Unlike you corporate guys, some of us have to make a living."

Jim pretended as if he were playing a small violin. "Ah, the old story of the battling entrepreneur."

Jason swung and his ball went straight and long, landing just a couple of feet from the cup. Jim stared, dumb-founded.

"Luckily, I was always better than you," Jason added as he slipped his borrowed club back into David's bag. David grinned and tapped him on the shoulder.

"And he's my partner for the day," said David. "You did say ten dollars a hole, didn't you Jim?"

"Ringer," said Jim, before stepping into his cart with Marc.

David and Jason stepped into the second cart.

"How are you feeling this morning?" said Jason. "That was a fantastic restaurant."

"L'Ami Louis. It's Bill Clinton's favorite. Though perhaps less so since his heart trouble."

"Those fries can't be good for anyone's heart. What was it, truffle they put on them?"

"They call it the French paradox. They eat all of this cheese, goose and duck fat, and drink a lot of red wine and somehow live forever. Meanwhile, we're all exercising and munching on lettuce leaves and dropping dead in our sixties."

"You must love it here."

"I do now. But France isn't exactly the land of the lotus eaters. All the stories about red tape are true. Even the simplest procedures, like setting up a bank account, seem to take forever."

"But come on. It beats Philly."

"Certainly does." The fresh air rose toward them from the forest of

Fontainebleau in great, clean gusts. "But you know, you miss some things. My job has this great title and all these ex-pat perks, but it's mostly ceremonial. The business units have the P&L authority. They set the strategy and make the products. I've just got to keep the locals happy, and assist with some key relationships."

"Nothing wrong with that. I'll show up at your ceremonies for a few months if you want to sweat the details of making door knobs for me."

"How's that going?"

"I shouldn't complain. We're getting into all kinds of other reproductions… vintage hardware…expanding our distributor network. Every day is different— marketing, supply chains, manufacturing—which is great. But it's exhausting too. You know, you have payroll to meet, accounts to collect, cash flow to manage. Sometimes it feels like there isn't a square inch left in my brain for anything else."

"Which is how it should be."

"Well, I wouldn't mind a family."

"Come on. You're the last of the red-hot swingers. It's why we're all so jealous."

"It gets a little old when you hit forty."

They looked over to where Marc was standing. He hacked his ball out of the rough to a nice lie to the right of the green. David stepped out of the cart, picked a 7-iron and let his ball bounce and roll to the edge of the green. Jim lofted his shot and it landed in the center of a bunker.

The four men walked toward the green. A birdie for Jason, pars for David and Marc, and a double bogey for Jim. "So, if you're not up for being the figure head of Carson-France," asked Jason after they got back in the cart, "then what are you going to do?"

"I got a call last night from the CEO of Carson. I used to work for her years ago. She wants to put my hat in the ring for a job running one of Carson's oldest business units."

"If nothing else, it's flattering. Congratulations. But what does 'put your hat in the ring' mean? Does that mean she's offering you the job?"

"What do I know?" David shrugged, "It's corporate speak. I guess it means there are other candidates. But I can't imagine she'd be calling me back to

Philadelphia if she wasn't serious."

"Do you want to do it?"

"I guess. It is a promotion after all."

"So you don't really want it?"

"I don't know yet. I'm still working off the red wine. It'd be great to run my own P&L. Maybe put myself in line for one of the top jobs. But you know, I spent three years in Eastern Europe, three in the Midwest. Maria has been faithfully trailing me around with the kids. And now we're here in Paris. OK, the work isn't challenging, but the life is great. Why would I give it up? To sell tweezers, trays and needles? To inch a little higher up the ladder? The good thing about these big companies is they're comfortable and they serve you up great opportunities. The bad thing is you're constantly involved in politics, and whether or not you move up is largely a matter of luck and who you buddy up to rather than competence. At least with your business, you either sell the doorknobs or you don't. And you control that."

"I wouldn't over-romanticize it, David. I have plenty of days when I wish I had your life. It's great when things go well at my company, but when things go wrong, it all ends up on my desk. Control is a wonderful thing. But the dark side is blame. I can't run for cover. I'm fully exposed, and I literally work my ass off."

"But isn't that why we all did this? So we could do something with our lives? Make things better? Not just waste our days collecting our paychecks."

"You really have been in France too long, David. You have too much time to think."

"All right you two-bit hustlers," said Jim as he pulled out his monstrous driver on the second tee. Wham! The ball travelled so far and fast, all four players shielded their eyes to try to see it soar off into the distance. Jim punched the air, like a victorious prize-fighter. "The gauntlet is now down, my friends."

"What do you know about Surgitec?" asked David.

"Surgitec? You want to talk about Surgitec on a morning like this?"

"Yes, I do."

"They're trying to break into France? Good luck with that."

"They're putting David's hat in the ring to run it," said Jason.

"I use their products," said Marc. "Trays, gloves, tools."

"Well that about sums it up," said Jim. "If you want to sell prophy kits to dentists, go for it."

"Don't worry. He's jealous," said Jason.

"Jealous? Me? I'm running bio-tech. I'm killing it over there."

"Seriously, Jim. You know Carson as well as I do. I want to know. As a friend, what do you think of Surgitec?"

"Man, I don't know. You've got it pretty sweet right here."

"Yes, but you know what these big territories are like. They're ambassadorial roles. To get to the top at Carson, you've got to run a business unit."

"Yeah, just not Surgitec. It's got no growth, no prospects. It's just a bunch of worn-out surgical supply salesmen and a couple of lousy manufacturing plants in Puerto Rico. You can't prove yourself there. You'll just be gathering dust, or worse, you'd be stuck running a dog."

"It's an $1.2 billion a year business, Jim."

"If it wasn't already part of Carson, there's no way in the world they'd acquire it. It's like some old piece of furniture. It's useful, you can sit on it, and no one wants to throw it away. But if the house burned down and it was destroyed, we'd all be thrilled to go buy something new."

"Still," said Jason. "There's a lot you can do with $1.2 billion on the top line."

"Maybe if it was your own company," said Jim. "But we're talking Carson here. If it's been decided that Surgitec is a foundation business and your job would be to supply cash and not suck up any investment capital, then you'd do that and not much else. You try to change things around and you'll get stomped on, especially with a business like Surgitec, where a lot of senior people have done time. Come on Marc. Take your shot."

"I think it sounds like a great opportunity," said Marc. "I buy Surgitec products and I can tell you it's a very old school business. I get these reps sitting in my waiting room a couple of times a quarter. The same pitch, the same sneaky attempts to get my attention. They bring me a box lunch, they leave me more samples than I have space to store, and litter my office with the latest and greatest in brochure-ware. They leave baseball tickets on my desk —every cheap gimmick they've learned in Sales 101. And then when I tell them I'm not going to pay what they're asking, they come back at me with discounts and payment plans. And I'm buying a few thousand dollars' worth of supplies, tops. Its seems like you'd have lots of ways to whip that business into shape."

"Fine. If you want to get into that kind of commodity business, be my guest," said Jim.

"Oil's a commodity, and those guys do pretty well," said Jason.

"Hey, Nicklaus. Just play the game."

The four men sat down at a table in the clubhouse with a view across the forest toward an eighteenth century chateau. The waitress poured out a bottle of white Burgundy.

"To Jim and the hundred and eighty dollars he just lost," said David.

"To Jim," said Jason and Marc, while Jim scowled in his seat.

"Not one hole," said Jim. "Not even one. You couldn't have let me have just one."

"What is it those corporate trainers you love to hire call this?" said Jason. "A learning experience? Or is this a teachable moment? One or the other."

"Steak frites, medium rare," said Jim, stabbing at the menu. The waitress took the other orders and disappeared. "You'll miss all this if you go back to Philadelphia. And I'm talking as a man who loves a cheese steak." He patted his large belly. "But I guess I can see it."

"You can?" said David.

"Yeah. Sure. You're in the prime of life. Do well at this, shuffle up the corporate ladder, and you can do Paris on your own dime in a few years. Stay where you are and you're hostage to your job. Isn't freedom what we're all after in the end?"

"Did losing at golf change your mind?"

"No, it's just…well, look. I'm in this supposedly high growth business unit, flooded with interest and investment, and we're still trying to figure out how on earth we're going to make money. That's its own kind of stress. At Surgitec, you know how you make money. You just have to figure out how to make more of it. Keep the whole ecosystem going, keep people in jobs. Stop the weeds from choking us from down below."

"So, you're thinking I can be like some aggressive chemical fertilizer."

"That's it. Like Elliot tells me, I'm the oak sapling, the thirty year project. You're the weed killer protecting the lawn."

"Shall we order some red for our main course?"

"Definitely," said Jason. "You've got a car taking us home, right?"

"Ah yes," said Jim. "The agony of corporate life."

After dropping his friends off at their hotel, David went home. As he opened the door to his apartment, he saw his wife, Maria, smiling broadly at the end of the hallway. He could hear his children playing in the family room while a Disney film burbled away in the background. Maria was clutching a letter.

"They've accepted him!"

"Who?"

"Tyler. They've accepted him at the American School." Of course, David realized. They'd been waiting to hear for weeks now. After a long application process and several rounds of interviews, their five-year-old son had been accepted into the most prestigious of Paris' English language schools. Given all they had gone through to get this far, it should have been cause for celebration.

David walked across the hall and took Maria's hand.

"We have to talk. I would have told you this morning, but you were still asleep when I left, but I have to fly back to Philadelphia on Monday night."

"What's happened?"

"Linda Thomas, our new CEO, wants to put me up to run a business unit."

"Where?"

"Just outside Philadelphia."

"You're kidding. We just got settled in here. It took us eight months to find this apartment, a year to get the kids into the right school…."

"I know. Nothing's confirmed yet. But I can't say no to the CEO. Let me just go and talk to them about it." Maria's head dropped. The letter was now crumpled in her hand.

"How much longer do we have to do this? I feel like I've been following you around forever. The boys need a home. They need friends, consistency. I need friends. Just some sense of the future, instead of this permanent merry-go-round.

I thought we'd be here four years at least."

"So did I. I didn't plan for this. The call came completely out of the blue. The good news is they must think I've been doing a good job. It would be my own $1.2 billion business unit, Maria. If I do well at that, the next stop is the very highest ranks of the company. It's what I've been working for all these years. What we've been working for."

"Where would we live?"

"In the city, if you'd like. Or somewhere out along the Main Line. At least we'll be closer to your family."

"That's a mixed blessing. All those French lessons, David. All for what?"

"Listen, nothing's finalized. All I'm doing is going for a talk. A talk, that's all."

Maria got up from the table without saying a word and disappeared into the kitchen. David followed her and stood in the doorway. Their nanny brushed past him with a chocolate crepe for the children. A bottle of wine was open on the counter. He couldn't remember if he had opened it last night. Maria poured herself a glass.

"You always say you work for us," she said, without turning to look at him. "That we are the reason you get up and go to the office."

"That hasn't changed."

"Well, if that's really the case, I'm asking you not to take whatever it is they're offering you. Let's just do the four years here we planned and then move on after that. I cannot spend my life bending everything to the whims of the Carson Corporation. It's not fair. All of this—the apartment, the car, the money—it's not worth all the change. It's time we put some roots down, David. High time. I'd understand this more if you were in your early twenties. We didn't have to worry about anyone or anything. But now, we have responsibilities. We can't just keep upping and leaving every time someone in the C-suite has a brainwave."

"I understand."

"If you understood, you wouldn't get on that plane on Monday. You'd say you're not interested right now, but come back in a couple of years."

"You know what would happen if I did that. It would be a permanent diversion from the path that I've tried so hard to stay on."

"You don't know that because you've never stood up to the company like that. You always do what they ask of you."

David felt a rage starting to boil inside him. But he checked himself. She was angry, and she had every right to be. He had to let her vent. The time would come to discuss this rationally. Now was not it. He stepped away from the door and went to their bedroom. He shut the door and sat on the edge of the bed. He replayed the message from the night before.

"Have a great weekend. Send my best to your family," Linda had said cheerily.

So much for that.

Chapter 4

In With The New

David pulled his rental car into the lot at Carson's headquarters. It was 6:45 a.m. and there were only a handful of other cars there. He parked and took a sip of his coffee. He hadn't been back to the US for three months, since his father's funeral in Detroit.

His dad had worked as a machinist for thirty years before retiring to a cabin on Lake Michigan. It was a good turn-out. About 150 people—former colleagues, fishing buddies. David's mother had spoken movingly about her husband, a quiet man, but a provider. Dependable. He was lucky to retire before the bottom fell out of the auto industry, but he never forgot those less fortunate. He spent a lot of time in retirement helping those who lost their jobs hold on to their health insurance and homes, and navigate all the paperwork with which the government buried those most in need. His only reward was seeing these people retain some of the dignity they had spent a lifetime striving to acquire.

Whenever David came home, he and his father would say little until they were out on the water, their hooks baited and ready to drop in the water. Then would come the question. "So what exactly is it you do, son?"

Every year the answer changed. One year, it was "marketing for hospital beds," the next "finance for the credit business unit." One time, his father had said to him, "all this rotating sounds like you're not going deep on anything." It's general manager training, he told his father. "I thought you got to be a manager if you were good at something. Never realized it was a separate skill."

There was no point arguing the point, David soon found out. Far better to admit defeat and spend the day watching their lines and drinking through the six pack of Pabst Blue Ribbon his father unfailingly brought out in a battered green cooler.

But his father's comments always lodged deep in his mind. What did a general manager actually do? And what if the company you worked for ceased to exist? A general manager couldn't fix a leaky pipe or paint a ceiling or repair a sputtering engine. He needed a corporation, a structure in which to manage. He could win respect for managing a training program that had nothing to do with the bottom line, or speaking good "corporate speak" at meetings. For his dad, the tools he made either worked or they didn't. If he was a fraction of a millimeter off, his work was a failure. At Carson, you could flush away millions without anyone noticing, much less caring. You were often rated more on criteria cooked up by the HR group rather than real business success.

David stepped out of the car, reached for his computer bag and swung it over his shoulder. The air was thick and muggy, the way it never was in France. By noon, it would be sweltering. The sprinklers were already working hard to keep the grassy expanses leading up to the corporate headquarters from turning brown.

The atrium of the Carson Corporation rose up twelve stories. The air was fresh and cool inside, an effect exaggerated by the cream-colored marble floor and walls. A giant pop art painting, forty feet tall, hung on the wall facing the reception.

"David Hewitt for Linda Thomas," he told the receptionist.

"I.D. please."

He handed her his corporate I.D. from France.

"Paris," she said as she typed in his details. "Lucky you. I've always wanted to go." She slid a special black badge across the desk, enabling David access to the executive suite. "Go through the nearest turnstile and the guard will show you up—twelfth floor."

"Thanks," he replied, while realizing that he had never before been cleared to access the top floor of Carson's headquarters.

He pushed through the gate and walked to the elevator, which whooshed him noiselessly upwards. Eighty-six degrees in Philadelphia, he saw on the screen above the buttons. Congress gridlocked. New housing starts down 14 percent. Some actress he'd barely heard of caught doing something ridiculous. Did anything ever change?

The elevator doors opened to reveal a stretch of tan carpet leading to a set of glass doors. He walked down and pushed on the door. It was locked. The door rattled as he pulled the handle and a secretary popped up from her desk and walked over to let him in.

"David Hewitt? Do come in and take a seat. Linda just called. She will be here in five minutes. Can I get you anything? Would you like a fresh cup of coffee?" She was staring at the stained paper cup in his hand.

"Thank you. That would be great." He sat down on one of the modern leather sofas outside Linda's office. He picked up a copy of the *Wall Street Journal*, but couldn't focus on the headlines. There were copies of *Forbes*, *Fortune*, and *The Economist* on the table as well, all in mint condition, unread. The secretary brought him his coffee in a white, china cup.

As David took his first sip, Linda came bursting through the door with a rousing "Good morning!" It seemed as though an entire group of people had just come in, except Linda was alone. "Did you see the governor's address last night?" she asked the receptionist. "The man looked terrified to me—" Suddenly, she noticed Hewitt.

"David, you made it. Thank you. How's France? I haven't been since my twenty-fifth wedding anniversary. We had dinner at this place…what was it called, Tally-ho…."

"Taillevent."

"That's it. Very frou-frou. Waiters hovering around us all the time. You know they love to say the French economy is too socialist, but whenever I visit, I think 'these are my kind of socialists.' You've got some coffee. Leave the rest of your things here. Come with me."

David got up and followed Linda down the corridor, past the other executive offices. The walls were lined with etchings by American artists all in blond, wood frames. As they reached the end, Linda turned.

"Morning, Ellen." David watched the matronly woman get up and hand Linda a file. "Thank you, Ellen. Meet David. He hates me already because I want to bring him back from Paris."

"I'd hate you too if you did that to me," said Ellen to David.

"Enough of that. David, come in and take a seat."

David looked around the sparsely furnished office.

"You ever do any sales, David?"

"I spent a year selling with the diagnostic equipment team."

"So you'll know that sales trick of going into an office and looking for a hook? Some way of engaging with your customer—the fishing photo, the kids, the sports memorabilia. I didn't intend it that way, but having nothing in your office doesn't offer much for your visitors to jabber about. I'm beginning to like it as it is."

Linda removed her jacket and hung it on a hook attached to an empty bookshelf. She set the file down on her desk and rocked back in her chair.

"How was your flight?"

"Fine. Air France."

"Good. At least it wasn't one of our American carriers. I'd kill myself before taking one of those long distance. The food is atrocious."

David laughed and took another sip of his coffee.

"You had a chance to look at Surgitec?"

"As much as I could."

"So I guess you know it's a dog of a business."

"Good revenue though."

"Good revenue but lousy margins, and the five year trend is just bad news following more bad news. It's not worth a damn on those terms. So what do you think? You reckon you could do something with it?"

"I don't know much about surgical devices."

"You don't need to—it's gloves, trays, needles. The company is sales, marketing, manufacturing, and distribution. Same things you've been doing elsewhere."

"Linda, I've got to tell you, it was not easy moving my family to France, and now that we're finally settling in—"

"Of course, of course, but that's not the point. I've always been impressed by you, David. Ever since you worked for me all those years ago. It takes a special kind of person to remain in this kind of corporate environment. You've done that. And I need people like that to help me give Carson a shot in the arm. You've read the rumors, I'm sure. That we're a takeover target. That shareholders are getting antsy. We need to perform, David. Quickly."

"I appreciate your faith, Linda—"

"I'm going to go out on a limb for you, David. For your career. You succeed with this and you'll have a clear path to the top of this company. You stay in France, you could be waiting for your pink slip when someone else takes over at Carson and realizes that Western Europe's a threadbare market that we should exit. Then it certainly won't be you making the decision about where to go."

"What about the other candidates?"

"If you say yes, there won't be any other candidates."

"And if I say no?"

"This is a great opportunity for you David. You're forty-three, right? And I'm giving you a shot at running a business with sales of over one billion dollars. And what's more, I'm giving you my support to put a boot in its rear. You should be dreaming of this kind of chance. The upside could be huge."

"But it's a foundation business, Linda. I thought you ran these businesses for cash."

"Sure. You could look at this as a well that's just about been siphoned dry. Or you could look at $1.2 billion in sales and four and a half percent ROCE and think that you could do better. About four times as good, in fact, if Surgitec is to remain in Carson's portfolio." She tapped the file on her desk. "I've done some back of the envelope analysis on Surgitec. I'd like you to do the same. Run the numbers and tell me what you think. Right now, its earnings are thirty to forty million on assets of nearly one billion dollars. To keep up with the rest of the company, its earnings should be a hundred and sixty million dollars."

David raised his eyebrows.

"I know. It's a lot. Quadruple earnings. But what are you in this for? To improve your wine collection?"

"Let me take a look. I need to talk to my wife."

"If you need help with anything back here, schools, homes, whatever you need. Don't worry about going through the usual corporate channels. Just ask Ellen. She'll help you out."

"Really?"

"Really. I want you here in a month. Your family can come later."

David picked up the file, hesitantly.

"What is it?"

"Why Surgitec?"

"When I have a multi-billion dollar company to run, you mean? Why am I getting in the weeds about who runs Surgitec?"

"Yes."

"You'll be in charge of twenty-four hundred people, David. Throw in their families, you'll have maybe seven thousand people depending on you. For each one of those, Carson isn't a multi-billion dollar corporation. It's a monthly paycheck. It's health insurance. It's a mortgage payment, a college fund. Of course, as an executive, I want to make some changes. I don't want anyone thinking that just because Carson is huge, it has places to hide. But I also want to do this to make sure those twenty-four hundred people have a future. It's not fair to keep people shackled to a business without trying to improve it. All you are doing is exposing them to risks they can't yet see. The risk of becoming obsolete, of being overtaken by a rival, or being bought out by another corporation that has no loyalty to them. It's my job and yours to look into the future and to protect these people. Make sense?"

"Perfect sense."

"When do you fly back to France?"

"Tomorrow morning."

"Call me Thursday then, after you've talked it over with your family."

The buzzer went. Linda pressed the button.

"Two minutes till the board meeting."

"I'll be right there."

They both got up. Linda rested her hand on David's shoulder as she ushered him out.

"We'll do great things."

Linda closed the door. David walked back to the reception area and picked up his computer bag. He pushed the elevator button to go down and exhaled. But just as the doors were closing a hand reached in.

"David. What a surprise."

"Elliot. Good to see you." The doors slid back open to let him in.

"How was Linda?"

"I'm sure you know much better than I do."

"She seems to think you'd be a good choice for Surgitec." David said nothing. "You don't have a background in supplies do you?"

"No."

"And France must be nice. Listen, David. A word of advice. Surgitec is a dying business. A young guy like you could get buried there. Stay four or five years more in Paris, and you'll still be in your forties. It's not a turnaround situation. Leave Surgitec to one of the senior guys. Your turn will come. At this point in your career, you want something high-growth. A real rocket. Keep doing the right things and that could be sooner rather than later. Jim's an old friend of yours, isn't he? In biotech? He's really proving himself there."

The elevator had reached the ground floor. "Think about it," said Elliot before stepping out into the now bustling lobby.

Bloody Mary, please," said David to the Air France flight attendant, "spicy." He leaned back into his seat and stared at the screen in front of him. The in-flight entertainment system had yet to start up, so the screen was just showing a floating bubble pattern. He gazed at it, his eyes following the multi-colored bubbles as they drifted across a blue sky. If this chance had come three years earlier, he would have snatched at it, no question. His own business unit, with its own P&L, 2,400 employees, and $1.2 billion in revenue. It was exactly the kind of chance you joined Carson for. It was what they trained you for. So why was he hesitating? There was his family, of course. But when you thought hard about it, it would be crazy to give up now, to stop in Paris after enduring so much to get where they were, so many moves, so many different homes, so much travel. What difference did one more make?

As for whether or not it was the right career move, he had the CEO urging him to take it. Not some mid-level HR staffer, but the CEO, calling him over and telling him this was his big move. Whenever younger executives came to him for advice, David always told them not to try to be too strategic about their careers. Just focus on each task given you, do it the best you can, and more, better tasks will follow. You could waste your life angling and politicking for certain opportunities, but the best insurance for a great career was just to be really good at whatever you did. And now what was he doing? Letting Jim and Elliot's words infect his thinking. What did they know? Neither of them were chief executive. Elliot had even botched his own chances of the top job through his own incompetence. But he was still a powerful figure at Carson, and a vengeful one, by all accounts. Cross him and he would never forget. Who was to say Linda would continue to stand by David over the next two years? What if she cut him adrift with this dog of a company and Elliot as his mortal enemy?

But what had really hooked him was what Linda had said about the people. David tried to imagine what his father would think of the opportunity. "Put that education to use in making and keeping jobs, in securing and expanding a viable business," he would have said. If that's what a general manager can do, that would be something he would have understood and been proud of.

Then he would have a dropped another line into the lake and waited for a fish to bite.

By the time David's taxi pulled up at his building in the 16th Arrondissement, it was midnight. He pulled his bag from the trunk, paid the driver, and went inside. He climbed the single flight to his apartment and turned the lock as quietly as he could. As he stepped inside, he saw Maria's outline sitting on the window ledge in the living room.

"You want to do this, don't you?" she said softly.

"Very much. Yes."

"Then let's do it."

He walked quickly over toward her and took her hand.

"Thank you. I know it's been hard…."

"It's OK. You've given us all an adventure. You've spoiled us. But I do just want one more thing out of Paris."

"Name it."

"We've never been up the Eiffel Tower."

"Is this Ellen?" David shouted over the strong wind blowing into him on the second floor of the Eiffel Tower. "David Hewitt here for Linda." He put his hand to the phone and said to Maria "You were right about not taking the elevator. The stairs were much better." He pointed down to their two children who were sitting on the ground, panting. Tourists milled all around them, taking photographs and gawping across Paris.

"David, great to hear from you."

"Linda, I am calling to say I'd love to take the job at Surgitec."

"Good move. I'll put your name up on Monday. There are a couple of other names in the running, but I'll argue for you forcefully."

"I still need to get things organized here…."

The line was dead.

Chapter 5

Where's My Computer?

Surgitec's headquarters were in Harleysville, Pennsylvania, a small town forty miles northwest of Philadelphia. It was a collection of low buildings put up in the early 1960s by a then famous architect. Carson took care to look after them; and for architectural students, they were regarded as a valuable time capsule, classic commercial buildings. A casual passer-by, however, might have wondered what all the fuss was about. As David pulled into the parking lot, the same thought crossed his mind.

Ten years earlier, David had attended a corporate training seminar at which a business school professor had given them a schedule for a week and told them to fill it out as if they had just taken over a business. Some people had returned it empty, saying they simply wanted to observe during their first few days, rather than come in all guns blazing. Others wrote up a schedule as if they had been doing the job for several months already.

The right approach, the professor had said, was to get out and meet as many people as possible, not just your staff, but also customers and suppliers. You only had a short window in which to make a first impression, before you became old news, or others began to define your image for you. David had done it in Paris, spending his first two months on the road around Western Europe, getting to know the people he would be doing business with. The experience had served him well. Whenever a problem arose, he could put a face to it.

Today, he would do the same thing. Come in at full tilt. Exude energy and optimism.

He crossed the lot and pushed open the heavy glass doors of the entrance. It was a clean, modest office building, very different from the swaggering corporate headquarters. On the walls were posters for new knee parts and IV systems. Three beige sofas sat along the wall facing the reception. The receptionists had not yet arrived. A security guard was manning the front desk.

"Good morning," said David, cheerfully. The guard looked at him and took a sip of coffee without saying a word. "I'm new here."

"You'll have to wait until nine a.m. then."

"My name is David Hewitt. My details should be all there."

The guard took a bite from his bagel and wearily closed his newspaper. He licked his fingers, rubbed his hands together and began tapping on the keyboard.

"Hewitt, you said?"

"Yes, David Hewitt."

The guard tapped in the name, using just one finger on each hand.

"I.D. please."

Hewitt handed over his Carson badge. The guard entered his details then pushed the card back over the counter along with a temporary building pass.

"Go through here and take the elevator to the third floor." The guard immediately went back to his newspaper. David paused for a moment, wondering if he should introduce himself. The guard's eyes drifted up toward him.

"Anything the matter?"

David smiled and shook his head. He walked on and swiped his pass. Just as he did, he heard the guard's voice.

"Just messin' with ya, Mr. Hewitt. I saw your picture in the company newsletter. Welcome to Surgitec."

Hewitt spun around. The guard was standing now, brushing crumbs off his blazer.

"I thought you might be from one of these outside security companies."

"No. Been here for twenty-two years."

"And what's your name?"

"Ernie Davis."

"Thanks for the welcome, Ernie." Hewitt turned then turned back. "Am I the first one here?"

"By about an hour and a half, I'd say."

Hewitt checked his watch. It was 7:30.

"No one shows up until nine?"

"Only the really eager ones."

"Good to know. Thank you."

"Hope I haven't got anyone in trouble."

"No, you haven't. I've just got a lot to learn."

David came out of the elevator on the third floor. To his left was a glass door etched with the word "Finance Department." To his right, one marked "Office of the Chief Executive." The flooring was a checkerboard of clean vinyl squares, and there were a couple more posters advertising Surgitec's products—tweezers, this time, and some sort of suture. David pulled the door to his new office. He pushed. He rattled it. He looked to either side to see if there was some sort of ID swipe pad. Nothing. He knocked hard then pressed his face up against the door to see if he could look further into the room. His breath left a semi-circle of condensation on the door. He wiped it off with his hand. He turned and saw a telephone in the other corner of the hallway. He walked over, picked it up, and heard a tone. He pressed 0. Within two rings, it was picked up.

"Security."

"Ernie, it's David Hewitt. My office is locked. Do you have the key."

"I'll have to get it. Give me five."

David hung up and walked back to his door. He grabbed his briefing notes from his attaché and rested his shoulder against the wall. He had spent the night before in his hotel room, highlighting the passages he found relevant, good and bad. The consistent top line versus the shrinking margins. The stable workforce versus the atmosphere of complacency, which seemed to envelop the business unit. He stared up at the ceiling tiles. Boy, if his wife could see him now, there was no way she would ever leave Paris. Slumped in a hallway, and locked out of his new office. Ah, the glamour of executive life.

The elevator slid open, and before David could right himself, a woman of fifty or so wearing a navy pantsuit bustled out.

"I am so sorry, Mr. Hewitt. I meant to be here before you arrived, but never thought you'd get here so early. George wasn't such an early bird, you see, so I suppose I got used to it. And the traffic this early, who'd have thought everyone got going so early? Anyway, I stopped off at Dunkin' and bought donuts for everyone so we can celebrate your being here at Surgitec. We're so happy to have you. We'll miss George of course, but it's so nice to have you, and we've all heard such good things." She pulled a key from her pocket and unlocked the top and bottom locks on the door. "I'm Marjorie Cleave, by the way, your executive assistant. Been at Surgitec twenty-six years. Know the place top to bottom. Come on in. It's always a bit musty in here after the weekend, but I'll throw open a couple of windows and it'll be fine."

David looked around. Three desks were arranged in a horseshoe in the hallway. Then a corridor ran down to the right.

"You're down at the end there," said Marjorie. "But wait here a moment."

Twenty feet beyond the window was a curtain of trees. It was like sitting up in the forest canopy. Marjorie turned the handles to wind open two of the windows. "We have to do this now, because by ten, it'll be too hot. Now, come with me."

David followed her down the hallway past the row of executive offices. The door to his office was open and Marjorie showed him in. "All yours."

It was as large as a good-sized living room. Two of the walls were floor to ceiling windows overlooking a stream and shaded by trees. At one end was an oak meeting table with six seats. Recently emptied bookshelves ran the length of one wall.

"We need to give those a proper dusting," said Marjorie. In the middle of the room was a sitting area, a cream sofa and two chairs, and at the end a modest desk, as if an afterthought to everything else in there.

"Where's my computer?"

"George never liked using a computer."

"What do you mean?"

"Well, I have a computer and whenever he needed to read anything, I'd print it out and bring it in to him."

"What about emails?"

"Oh, he had a Blackberry and he used that. And he had a laptop that he used from time to time. He just didn't want a big screen cluttering up his desk. He said it got in the way when he was trying to talk to people. Such a people person, George."

"I'm going to need one, I'm afraid. Could you have one brought up here as soon as you can?" David set his briefcase down the empty desk. "And once you're ready, could we sit down and go over my schedule for the week?"

"Of course, I'll be right back." Marjorie left the door open and disappeared down the corridor. David noticed the expensive beige wall-to-wall carpet and the exotic rug in the center of the room. There was even a large, antique globe next to the sofa. The kind you could spin. What was this? 1975? A chief executive of a surgical supplies company with an antique globe?

He sat down in the high-backed leather chair, another totem from an earlier era of management. There was a single drawer in the desk. He pulled it open and saw an envelope addressed to him. He took it out, tore it open and began to read.

Dear David,

Welcome to Surgitec! You are one lucky guy to be sitting where you are now. It has been the great privilege of my life to run this business unit of Carson - to work with such remarkable employees and customers to make Surgitec what it is today.

I've had some of my happiest days in the office where you find yourself. Meeting fascinating people and enabling such incredible researchers, manufacturers, and salespeople to go out into the world with all of our wonderful products, to help people get well. That, I guess, is the core of it all. What we make helps people at moments of their greatest distress. When they are lying on a hospital table expecting the worst, Surgitec's products are there to help everything go smoothly.

Not that there aren't lots of people ready to criticize us. They say we're old-school. That what we do can be done better, cheaper. That the Chinese are going to eat our lunch. But you know what, David? They've been saying that for as long as I was at Surgitec. And it's never happened. Why? Because when it comes down to it, our customers don't just buy on price. Turns out they like to know that we're here for them. They like to buy from people they know, like, and trust.

Not so long ago, you may have read about it
in the newspaper, there was an explosion at a
big, new electricity plant here in Pennsylvania.
The workers were testing a gas line and it blew
up. Fifty-three men were injured, many seriously.
Six died. On the day it happened, the nearest
hospital was overwhelmed. The manager called me
personally to ask for a delivery of supplies.
I got on the phone to the warehouse, called in
the salesman who serviced the account, and we
drove over ourselves - on a Sunday morning! I
called several other people at the company who
lived locally, and they all showed up, bringing
coffee and sandwiches for the families waiting
at the hospital. We provided 40 free cellphones
for people to use and laid out a shuttle service
for families and hospital workers for the whole
next week. Our employees were the drivers, VPs
of sales and marketing, the head of R&D, guys
from manufacturing. I've never been more proud of
this company and my team. Do you ever think that
hospital, or group of hospitals, is ever going to
buy from China?

I don't.

Surgitec is more than a company. It is a
trust. A place where people find meaning in their
lives. I hope you can continue that tradition.

You'll probably have met Marjorie by now. She
is a treasure. Her husband worked for Surgitec
for 30 years, before he died last year. They were
celebrating their 25th wedding anniversary in
Florida. He had a heart attack on a fishing boat.
She won't tell you about it, but I thought you
should know. She deserves only the best.

Two final things:

- the hot water faucet in the men's room
  sticks, and

- my lowest score at the Winged Eagle Club

```
    was a 74. Beat that!

    Have fun, David. You're a lucky guy, and I
envy you having these years at Surgitec ahead of
you.

    Call if you get lost,

    George
```

He stuffed the letter back into its envelope just as Marjorie came back into his office.

"I sent an email to IT asking for a computer. They don't get in until around nine thirty generally, but they stay an extra half an hour in the evening. It's something to do with how these millenials work. Someone in HR read an article saying that kids born since nineteen eighty like to come in later and stay later. It makes them feel more respected, I think. Anyway, they're generally pretty reliable, so you should have your computer today." She set down a white mug, emblazoned with the Surgitec logo and filled almost to the very top with black coffee.

"I don't know how you like it yet, so I brought everything." She dropped a handful of creamer and sugar packets on the table. "George liked his milky and sweet. But we had to put him on the artificial sweetener recently. High cholesterol. How do you like your coffee?"

"Black is fine." He took a sip. It was scalding and bitter. He put the mug back down, trying not to wince. "Now, my schedule."

"I've got it right here. Today and tomorrow I've left wide open, so you can find your feet. Then on Wednesday, there's a salesman of the year lunch at the Club. On Thursday, you're expected in downtown Philadelphia for a conference on managed healthcare organizations. Friday morning, is 'bring your daughters to work day'; it's a big deal round here, so I thought you'd want to be involved somehow in that. George used to do a treasure a hunt in the parking lot."

"Do I have any meetings set up with my direct reports?"

"Whom did you have in mind?"

"All the functional VPs—sales, marketing, finance, etcetera...."

"Well, Barry Johnson, the head of sales, is in Atlanta this week. It's the

Health Trust Invitational. Bob Grieve, who runs manufacturing, is due back from Puerto Rico tomorrow, I think. He's been down there looking at one of the plants. Anyone else?"

"Finance? Marketing? R&D?"

"Oh, they should be around. Would you like me to set something up?"

"Yes. And for Bob Grieve. Also, would you mind getting me Barry Johnson's number?"

"You're going to call him down in Atlanta?"

"Yes."

"This tournament's a big deal for Barry. He came in runner-up last year. George used to go with him, but this year, he's down there all alone."

"People seem to play a lot of golf around here."

"George used to say more business gets done on the golf course than in the office."

It was all David could do not to reply, "it shows." But instead, he smiled.

"If you could arrange for me to meet all of my VPs over the next couple of days, I'd appreciate it. I feel it's important that we all get off on the right foot."

"Of course."

"Also, you should know that my wife's name is Maria. So if she calls, please put her straight through."

"Anything else?"

"No. That's everything for now. Oh, one more thing, did George leave me any files? Anything I need to read?"

"Heavens no! George was a terrific delegator. He used to say that effective delegation was the mark of great leadership. He left all the file-keeping to others. He used to say that a clean desk shows an organized mind."

Or an empty one, thought David, as Marjorie rose and left the room.

Chapter 6

Expensive Systems, Cheap Motels

"Marjorie said you'd like to see me…Andy Butler, finance."

David swung his feet off the desk and rose to greet his guest. He glanced at his watch, 9:03 a.m.

"Yes, of course, Andy. Thanks for stopping by. Listen, there's nothing in here besides chairs and dusty bookshelves. Let's go to your office."

Andy was shorter than David, with a belly protruding over the top of his khakis. He wore a blue shirt and rimless glasses. What was left of his thinned out hair was light brown and combed backward across his scalp.

"We're down a floor if you don't mind."

"No problem at all. I should get to know the building. Is there a staircase we could take?"

"Sure. I should take it more often. Lose some of this." He patted his stomach. "As my doctor is always telling me, spreadsheets aren't exercise."

"How long have you been here, Andy?"

"At Surgitec? Or Carlson?"

"Both."

"Ten years at Surgitec, fifteen at Carlson. Spent a few years at HQ before being sent over here. I became CFO two years ago."

"How's it been?"

"My father worked for Surgitec, in accounting, so I grew up around the company. I used to come to this building when I was a boy to visit him. It's

EXECUTIVE
TEAM

Meet David and his Leadership Team
On-Line at www.smashing-silos.com

amazing how little has changed. Same culture, good people. Steady as she goes."

Andy opened the stairwell door and they went through, clattering down a flight of concrete steps to the second floor. As they emerged into the hallway, David noted that it looked exactly the same as upstairs. Same colors on the wall, same linoleum floor, same posters on the walls. It was egalitarian if nothing else. Andy's office was a couple of doors to the right. They passed a coffee station, where several employees were talking about their weekends and passing around a box of donuts. David nodded at them and they fell silent.

"Take a seat," said Andy, as he settled into his Aeron chair on the other side of his desk, which was covered with tidy stacks of reports.

"How old?" asked David, pointing to a photograph of children on the desk.

"Six, nine, and twelve."

"Lucky you. We've got two, a few years younger."

"Everyone says it passes so quickly. And the amazing thing is, it does."

"So, Andy, what's the view from in here?"

"Aside from the parking lot?" David laughed at the lame joke. "The business seems to be in good shape, we're selling well and revenue keeps rising...."

"No, not the whole company. Finance."

"We went through a big ERP implementation and finally came out of it earlier this year. It really cleaned up a lot of the reporting. Made our jobs a lot easier. We closed our books right on time this year. It meant we could gather information from all across the company much more quickly."

"A successful ERP implementation. You don't hear that very often."

"Oh, it was the second in seven years. It took us a while to get it right, but I think we did this time."

"How much did it cost?"

"Oh, you don't want to know that...both rounds?"

"Yes, and the latest project."

"Maybe eighty-five million dollars total. The latest round, let me see." He swung his chair round and picked a file off a table behind him. "All in, $35,328,000."

David exhaled sharply. "Now there's a business."

"We used different vendors each time," said Andy

"What happened to the old systems?"

"We use parts of them. Some of the old applications were so intertwined with Carson's legacy systems that we just couldn't imagine replacing or rebuilding them, so we integrated those data feeds into the new ERP. That's the tough thing about modernizing. Feels like you can never get rid of the old. It was a bit of a patchwork at first, but it's working better now."

"Just better, or well?"

"It's easier for us to pull the regional and business unit results on a weekly and monthly basis so we can file our quarterly reports in a timely manner. It makes it easier to forecast as well."

"But?"

Andy stepped up, walked around his desk and closed the door.

"You really want to know the problem?"

"It's my first day on the job, Andy. I want to know everything."

"The problem with this company is it doesn't know the value of a cent, let alone a nickel or a dime." The jolly Andy of a minute earlier had been replaced by a hard-faced bean counter. "You look at our competitors; their costs are ten percent to fifteen percent lower than ours. In our business, there's not much you can do about pricing. We sell commodity goods. Our customers have been with us for years. You can't go upping prices on them. They'll get angry and leave. But you can cut costs. And you know where it starts? Sales. Last year, I tried to cut down on corporate travel expenses. Our guys were taking first class everywhere and staying wherever they liked. Our West Coast rep insists on staying in the Ritz Carlton, and because he was an old friend of George, no one stopped him."

"What did you do?"

"So, on my own initiative, I called around to hotel groups to get a better corporate rate. You know, at Wal-Mart, even the most senior executives share motel rooms. Motels. They stay in motels. And share the rooms. So I got a great deal set up with Days Inn. Nice hotels, clean rooms, some have pools. I've stayed with them with my own family. I got a bulk deal, a certain number of nights per year for our employees. What happens? The sales guys go running to George, as if I've just stolen their commissions, and George tells me to kill my plan. It's destructive for the sales team's morale."

"What else have you tried?"

"You've been at Carson a while. You know what the sales guys get away with. Submitting receipts from restaurants with names that sound a lot like strip clubs saying they had to take a group of doctors out. It's outrageous."

"You sound jealous, Andy." Andy laughed, awkwardly.

"We've tried everything they say in the books. Asking people to print on both sides of the paper. Encouraging them not to use their mobile phones for personal calls…"

"And you didn't move the needle."

"Right…not even a little bit."

"So what are your biggest numbers? I'm guessing the paper issue isn't guzzling up our gross margin."

"You could start with R&D. That was another of George's sacred cows. They think they have a divine right to eight percent of revenue. It should be down at five percent or six percent, and perhaps even that number should be reviewed each year depending on what they're coming up with over there in the mad scientists' lab."

"Are our competitors down at six percent?"

"Or lower. We even have a competitor that brags about being "last to market, but first in price." They just rip us off and wait for the lawsuit, which rarely comes. The whole thing needs to be tightened up and we need to be much more aggressive about defending the products that really do belong to us. In any case, they've been calling us a 'foundation business' ever since they did that big strategy project up at corporate. No one is looking to us to innovate."

"That's what I keep hearing," said David, "that we're a foundation business, which, as far as I can tell, means we just keep chugging out the cash and no one pays us too much attention to us. How do you feel about that?"

"I think we can do much better on cost, David." Andy rested his elbows on his desk and leaned forward. David heard several pings as email landed in Andy's inbox. "To be honest, I was really happy to hear about your appointment. We need some new blood around here, someone to look at all these costs with fresh eyes. To see if they're justified. With this new ERP, we have the systems in place to really ratchet down on costs, to make sure we're getting value out of every dollar we spend."

David could feel Andy's eyes drilling into him. It was strange how affable he seemed at first. A long way from the fire-breathing cost accountant now sitting across the table.

"Fascinating. Will you send up any interesting work you have on what you're saying. It would be good to see this in cold, hard numbers."

"I'd be delighted to," agreed Andy.

"One more thing."

"Sure." Both men were standing now.

"My wife is going to be arriving from Paris in a month or so. We're going to be staying in a hotel until we find a house. So, just to check. The Days Inn plan was killed?"

"Never meant it for senior guys like you, big guy," said Andy, guffawing and blushing. "Only for the regular sales guys. Course not the top executives."

"Good, because I don't think she'd ever forgive me for bringing her back from Paris if she had to stay in a motel."

"Forget I ever mentioned it," said Andy. "She'll love it here."

David stepped back into the corridor. The group he had seen chatting by the coffee machine were now at their desks. All he could hear was the muffled sound of keyboards drifting up from cubicles and the hum of air conditioning. The two meeting rooms opposite Andy's office were empty, but there were still a few tired looking two-by-twos sketched up on the white boards.

He couldn't quite put his finger on it yet, but there was a malaise about the place.

Maybe it was just finance, he thought, as he pulled open the staircase door and bounded back upstairs.

A large rear-end in jeans greeted David as he walked back into his office. Marjorie was standing behind his desk.

"Over to the right a bit. Yes, there you go. Drop the wire through there." She looked up and saw David in the doorway. "It's the computer you asked for. They're going to get you all setup—hardware, software, the whole lot. Aren't you, Drew?" The large figure bent over his desk straightened up and turned around.

He was young, early twenties, with a goatee, a black ski cap, and a black Eagles sweatshirt.

"Give me five more minutes and you'll be all set. You can get into the Carson system using your existing password, but you'll need to set up a new one to access Surgitec's system."

"I can never remember all these passwords."

"Me neither. They should just have one, but you know how it is. Usual corporate stuff. Too many systems, nothing talking to each other. Do you have a Blackberry, Sir? You need one?"

"I guess I'll need to replace my French one. But it works for now."

"Yeah, but you'll be paying global roaming charges. I'll get you a local one."

"How many of you are there in IT, Drew?"

"Depends. Right now…sixty…seventy. During big implementations, we go up to a hundred or more. And that's just here at headquarters."

"You always worked here?"

"Yes, Sir. Since college. Then I do programming in the evenings for all kinds of customers. You know, websites, corporate stuff…then for fun, music and gaming. Got customers all over the world these days." Drew tapped away at the keyboard until the screen sprang to life. "Here you go. Welcome to Oz."

"How did George do without this?"

"I've got no idea. Old school, I guess."

The Carson logo flashed up. David entered his details on the log-in screen. He was then asked which company he wished to sign into.

"Use your Carson ID. Then you get to set a Surgitec password."

He typed in his ID again. Now for a password. A single image pushed to the front of his mind. He typed the letters: "Eiffel4." The four of them, him and Maria and the kids, the wind blowing into their faces, the whole of Paris laid out below them.

The word Surgitec now appeared, ricocheting across the screen. The toolbar had options for employees, administrators, and customers.

"You have access as an administrator and an employee," said Drew. "That will allow you to see pretty much all we have on the front end."

"Can I see sales forecasts and pipelines?"

"That's all held on a separate system, which is only accessible to sales."

"I'd like to be able to see it."

"They bring all the data to the monthly sales meetings," said Majorie.

"I'd like to be able to see it in real time."

"That's not how they do it," confirmed Drew

"How do they do it?"

"I'm not an expert on this," said Drew. "But I think the salespeople have a filing deadline every two weeks when they have to input their activity charts and sales figures, and then that data is used to build the kind of charts you're talking about."

"So there's nothing live. If a sale gets made, we don't find out until a couple of weeks later, maybe."

"That's the way it's always been done."

"What about the transaction records? Where are they held?"

"In the ERP system. But finance controls that. It's not visible from here."

"How about pricing? Can I see what each customer is paying?"

"Well, I guess you could look up invoices in the ERP if we got you a password, but then you'd have to have training in the special programming code that the system uses."

David thrust himself back in his seat.

"So what can I do from this portal?"

"You can see the menu from the cafeteria." David flashed a scowl.

"I'm kidding. You can see the company directory. You can get access to your pay slips, healthcare information, pensions. There's the newsletter. And all the filings we have to make are here. HR can give you a code so you can see people's performance reviews."

"But nothing on sales, pricing, manufacturing.... And what about profit and loss statements? Is there any kind of financial dashboard?"

"Oh, there's this cool webcam feature—wait," he made a few keystrokes, "look, this is our plant in San Juan. You can watch it live." David peered at a few blurry figures moving around a large warehouse, picking items from a conveyor belt and arranging them in packing crates.

"This is not very revealing."

"It was part of a plan to create tighter integration of our geographically dispersed business units," said Marjorie. "It made Puerto Rico seem not so far away."

David puffed out his cheeks.

"Look, I'd like to be able to see what the heads of sales, manufacturing, and finance see. I'd like to see their data as soon as they see it. Is that possible?"

"It's possible," said Drew.

"Good. Then please make it happen. Today. Marjorie, what's the matter?" She was chewing hard on her pencil.

"It just that…doesn't matter. It's none of my business."

"Of course it's your business. What is it?"

"It just doesn't seem very trusting, that's all."

"I understand. But no one should see it that way. I'm trying to understand this company as best I can, as quickly as I can, and having access to the right data is going be a big part of that. If anyone objects, tell them to come and see me. I'll be more than happy to explain myself."

Chapter 7

This Is All Very Impressive

It took David just ten minutes to drive out to the R&D unit, which was housed in a large steel building, surrounded by high gates, behind an Applebee's. He swiped his pass and the barrier swept up, allowing him through. A gaunt man in gray slacks and a white shirt, with curly, salt and pepper hair was waiting for him in the parking lot. David pulled up beside him and opened his window.

"You must be Larry."

"And you must be David. Very good of you to squeeze us in like this on your first day."

"I'm not squeezing you in at all. It was important for me to come and see you. Thank you for sparing the time. You must be very busy." Larry shrugged.

"You can leave the car over there, where it says 'reserved.'" David parked and walked over to Larry, who was rolling a set of keys round and around his index finger. "I thought we'd start with a tour of the lab. Then we can go up to my office and talk, if you'd like."

"Sounds great. Let's see what you've got."

The warehouse covered around ten thousand square feet. On the main floor were several islands of worktables surrounding testing areas where prototypes could be vigorously tested. There were glass-walled rooms along one side containing larger pieces of machinery. On another side were sterile labs. About fifty scientists were working on this floor, half in white coats, the others in ordinary working clothes. There were banks of computers at every desk and

EXECUTIVE TEAM — Meet David and his Leadership Team On-Line at www.smashing-silos.com

cables running all along the floor. Running around the building at first-floor height were offices, which looked down onto the laboratory floor. Everyone and everything was visible in here, which David immediately liked. You could see people as they moved from their desks or emerged from their offices. You could hear them as they walked along the metal gangways overhead.

David saw a complex ball and socket device lying on one of the lab tables.

"What's this?" he asked Larry.

"We're experimenting with a new material for hip replacements."

"Do we already do hip replacement parts?"

"No. But it's a high value business if we can get into it. We're taking what we know about these materials and trying to apply that knowledge. It would be great if we could crack the hip market. It's already big and growing. The longer people live, the likelier it is they're going to need new hips. It would take Surgitec into a very new market. Over here, we've got some new implement trays. They're made of steel, but lighter than anything else on the market. Feel it." David picked one up. It was as light as a sheet of paper.

"Wow."

"And then we're making these tweezers, with a new flexible material, which we think gives surgeons greater control in complex procedures. We're looking to make them in various lengths for different situations."

As they walked the floor, David was impressed by the variety of what he saw and the engagement of the workers. It was all he had imagined an industrial laboratory could be.

"We do work with blood over there in the sterile labs," Larry went on. "We're constantly trying to improve the absorbency of our pads, bandages and so on. The faster they can soak up blood, while leaving the patient still feeling dry, the better. But it's one of those challenges that we keep on chasing. I don't think we'll ever be done with that one."

"So how do you decide on which projects to pursue?"

"Come upstairs." David followed Larry up the clattering metal stairs to his office, a modest room overlooking the lab floor. It contained a desk, two chairs and two filing cabinets. On the walls were three degree certificates, bachelor's and master's in engineering from Cornell, and a PhD in applied medical engineering from MIT. On the desk was one of the largest computer screens David had ever seen. Larry noticed him staring at it.

"Big screens are supposed to be great for productivity. Bill Gates works on two huge screens. Come and take a look." David stepped round to Larry's side of the desk. Five separate browser windows were open and fully visible, as well as Larry's email. The browser windows were open to academic and popular science journals. New emails hit the inbox every few seconds. "You don't have to keep opening and closing windows. It's much more efficient this way. Take a look at this." A new window opened to show a dynamic spreadsheet with dates along the top, a long list of products down the left side, and multi-colored bars stretching from left to right. "These are all our new products and the bars represent where we are with them, whether they're still in the research phase, prototyped, tested, approved, or already in manufacturing."

"But there are hundreds of them."

"The majority are modifications to existing products, often custom versions for specific customers. The rest are new products that we hope to commercialize one day."

"Tell me about some of your successes."

Larry sat back in his chair and whistled.

"We've had a few. Not long ago, we tweaked a new IV system for a hospital group in south Texas. They hire a lot of nurses down there that were trained in Latin America. They're used to a slightly different system, so rather than having to retrain the nurses, we just adjusted the system."

"How many did you sell?"

"Seventy or eighty, I think."

"What was the revenue?"

"You know, I'm not sure. Sales doesn't often report that kind of information to us."

"Do you know how much it cost you to do the work?"

"Four or five technicians, over a couple of weeks. Fifty thousand to a hundred thousand dollars maybe—tops. It was a small job, but the hospital was thrilled. Said it really improved productivity."

"Do you have the name of the device?"

"Sure. It was the IV X6780 Delivery System. We were very proud of it." David jotted down the information.

"Anything else."

"Oh, so many. We recently made a minute adjustment to a set of dentists' mirrors, you know the kind they put into your mouth to look around when you go for an appointment. It was a question of thousandths of millimeters but we're told it made a big difference. Then there are the classics. The kidney shaped surgical trays, the nylon suture materials, the sterilized scrubs, touch sensitive gloves for surgical work, the list goes on and on. Let me show you something." He pulled out a heavy green file and dumped it on the desk. "Take a look at these. These are letters from physicians all around the United States and the world thanking us for our work. We have hospitals like Brigham and Women's Hospital in Boston, the Mayo Clinic, Columbia Presbyterian in New York, really the best of the best." David opened the binder and glanced through the letters, each one contained in a plastic sheath, like holy relics. They were indeed gushing, full of gratitude and praise for Surgitec's products. He stopped at one from the head of surgery at Beth Israel Hospital in Los Angeles.

"We have tried other products, and yet we keep returning to Surgitec," read the letter. "No other company offers your level of service and innovation. Nothing is too minor for your attention. Your determination to do the best for us and for our patients far exceeds that of your competitors. We view you as our trusted partner in delivering the very best healthcare to our patients. Thank you for all that you do."

"This is all very impressive, Larry. Were you always in commercial research?"

"No. Only the past seven years. Before that I spent almost sixteen years at the Salk Institute in San Diego pursuing advanced medical devices research with a group of professors I got to know at MIT."

"What brought you back to the east coast? Most people I know in San Diego never want to leave."

"My parents live in Princeton. My Dad was a mathematician at the Advanced Studies Institute there. They were getting older and my mother fell ill, so I needed to be here."

"How are they doing now?"

"My mother passed away a couple of years ago. My dad's fine. He lives with us now, with me, my wife, and our kids. He has serious kidney trouble. In fact, there are a lot of Surgitec products used to help in his treatment. That means a lot." He pulled out a photograph of a young man looking remarkably like Larry standing next to Albert Einstein. "It's from when my dad first got to Princeton as a grad student. Einstein was still there." David picked it up and smiled.

"Incredible. You ever meet him?"

"No. Too young. But pretty amazing, huh?"

"Definitely. So, Larry, what I'd love to have from you is some kind of product pipeline. A sense of what you've got coming out of here that could hit the market in the next year, three years, and five years."

"No problem. It'll be a long list."

"That's great. Also, if you have any idea of the market size for the new products—"

"Oh, that's an issue for marketing," Larry interrupted. "They never let us get involved in those types of discussions."

"Fine. I'll bring it up with them. And then perhaps we can sit down together with them and sales and talk through what we can look forward to." He saw Larry wince. "What's the matter?"

"Corporate made us do one of those group sit-downs a couple of years ago. George agreed never again."

"Well, I hope you'll indulge me. I'm new here, so I need to do things formally before we can decide the best way to proceed in the future."

"Of course. Totally understand. A full list of products in the pipeline. You'll have it in the next couple of days. I'll get my guys together and we'll hash this out. You know, a lot of our best stuff is in here," he said tapping his head. "Then we crank it out when we think we're ready. So I'll try to get that down as well."

"Why don't we have two separate lists then. Products in physical R&D and great ideas for the future."

"Sounds fair. Hey, listen; do you play golf?" What was it with this place and golf, wondered David. "Try this." Larry handed him a silver tee. "It's made of titanium. You can whack the hell out of it. It won't break or even bend. We made it from left over materials we had after working on these new splints for people with bone fractures. The splints ended up being too expensive and not materially better than what's already on the market, but some of the guys thought they might try Nike or Callaway with this thing."

David peered at it.

"Just make sure Surgitec gets its piece of the royalties." Larry looked panicked for a moment, before David smiled. "You could probably make more off this than off a lifetime of making knee joints. Tells you something about the world, doesn't it?"

David pushed himself out of his chair, tucked his notepad in his pocket and walked out of the office. Larry followed him out to the parking lot.

"So, I'll wait for that list and perhaps we can have that meeting with the three departments early next week."

"Sure. Definitely. Absolutely," said Larry.

As David pulled out onto the small road leading away from the R&D center, he could only think one thing: golf tees.

Marketing occupied the ground floor of a building adjacent to the one where David worked. The offices were encircled by a wooden veranda, giving it the feel of a kids' summer camp. Inside, though, was a typical cubicle farm. Laura Chan's office was in the corner overlooking the stream, which ran past Surgitec's headquarters. She had run marketing for eighteen years, and the building reflected her personality. It was clean, orderly, and quiet. Surgitec posters, all perfectly hung, lined the walls. Seeing them altogether like this, you could see the creative sensibility behind them, the same fonts, colors, and graphics used year after year with only the slightest modifications. There was not a spare inch on the bookshelves. The books and journals were organized by subject and date of publication. An Italian coffee machine, far more elaborate than the humdrum filter coffee makers in the main building, sat on a counter in the staff kitchen, beside a stack of white espresso cups.

"Let me make you one," said Laura, grabbing a cup and turning a handle on the machine. "You probably had some great coffee in Paris. I went there with my family a couple of years ago. We stayed just outside the city in Le Vesinet with friends who work in marketing at Microsoft, but we went in and had some great meals. Did you have a favorite restaurant?"

"I used to take friends to L'Ami Louis. You knew you'd get the classic French experience."

"Sure, surrounded by Americans."

"Yes. OK. I'll give you that."

"We found these amazing little places in the back streets. Really authentic." She yanked at the machine and pressed a button. Viscous coffee started to dribble out of the machine. They watched it coat the bottom of the cup. When it was done, Laura passed it to David. "Best cup of coffee in Harleysville." David tasted it. It was like licking the inside of an old oil pan. "Let's go to my office." David followed Laura through the maze of cubicles, where employees worked shielded from the world by enormous sets of headphones. As if they might have to step out at any moment and direct airplane traffic. The average age seemed to be younger than in the rest of the building.

"Take a look at this," said Laura, passing David a magazine. "It's a prototype. A contract publishing company pitched us on the idea of doing our own magazine, a couple of times a year, to explain the company and our products to our customers. They did this for free. I'm thinking about it. It'd cost us about one hundred fifty thousand dollars an issue." David leafed through the glossy pages. Laura looked eagerly for his reaction.

"Do you think it would be worth it?"

"It would certainly be great for the brand. No doubt about it."

"So, tell me about the brand. How do you think about it?" Laura leaned forward on her elbows and extended her palms toward David.

"Surgitec's brand is a huge asset for this company. Because many of our products are commodities, people make the mistake of thinking price is all that matters. They couldn't be more wrong. Imagine if that were the case in the cola business. Why would anyone buy Coke if they can get a supermarket owned brand for less? It's the same with us. You can buy one of our rivals, but you don't get our brand value. Doctors want it and patients look for it. Our surveys tell us so. Wait there a moment." Laura got up and left the room. She returned thirty seconds later holding a black onyx pyramid with a golden star on top. "We won this for our most recent advertising campaign—Wellness Matters. It's the

American Advertiser award for best healthcare campaign."

"Congratulations."

"It was a collaboration with Baker Holman, our agency in Philadelphia. We've been working with them for twenty years now. They understand us and we've got our process down cold."

"When's the last time you put the advertising out to bid?"

"Not in my time here. We've never had to. Baker Holman gets what we do. That kind of mutual understanding would take years to develop with a new agency. Plus, we've had great success together. This isn't our first award."

"How do you measure the value of the brand?"

"What we try to measure is awareness. How many people know about us and what they think of when they hear our name. There are some great companies that do this kind of measurement work. What they tell us is that, in our space, we're a highly-respected, deeply-trusted name. That goes a long way in healthcare."

"Are there any financial metrics," probed David.

"You would expect a big premium if anyone wanted to acquire us! But really, it's tough to put a hard number on the value of the brand. But put it this way. If you were to set up a surgical supplies business today, what do you think it would take to develop a business and a reputation like ours? You could be just another generic supplier. But to build the kind of repeat business and to win customers like we do, that takes time and investment. It's why we take the time to work with customers, especially our overseas distributors, to get our packaging right," continued Laura.

"Different markets demand different packaging. You can't use the same packaging in Mexico, for example, that you do in the United States. It's not just changing the text to Spanish; it's about creating a visual that will appeal to the local market. We're constantly working with R&D to design new packaging and graphics for our products. Sales then gives us grief for holding up the supply chain, but I can't tell you enough, David, this stuff really matters. Our customers tell us so. And that's what it all comes down to, right? Keeping the customer happy."

"Do you have a minute, Laura," came a voice from the doorway.

"Of course, Zach, come in. This is David Hewitt, the new CEO of Surgitec. Meet Zach Klein, our head of graphic design."

"I'm sorry to disturb you. I can come back later."

"No problem. What have you got?"

"I wanted you to take a look at our new designs for the syringe packets."

"David, you're going to love this. Zach and his team have been working on these for, how many weeks is it, Zach?"

"Since March, so about nine weeks."

"OK, then let's see." Zach flipped over a large drawing board to reveal a few different versions of the same syringe. One had a purple tint, another green, one had the syringe pulled open, others had it pushed shut. Laura stepped up for a closer look.

"This is brilliant work, Zach. Brilliant." She invited David to stand with her to get a closer look at the designs. "Look at this. The syringes are filled to different levels in these two. It's a big debate in our profession whether customers prefer to see syringes empty or full, and if full, how full. Some people think it's best to show the devices in action; others, like them in a passive state. To make sure, we do both. Zach, which one are you leaning toward."

"Since this is for the Latin American market, I'm leaning toward this one, with the purple tint and half full."

"Which countries will this be going to?" asked David.

"Central America—Costa Rica, Venezuela, Guatemala…" said Laura. "And one other. Which one, Zach?"

"Ecuador," added Zach.

"How much do we sell in those markets?" said David.

"I think all in, we do about three to four million dollars."

"For syringes or all our products?"

"All our products."

"So for syringes. What's the market size?"

"This year? We did look at this. It was around four hundred thousand dollars, but it's growing. We've categorized this as high potential, which is why we put Zach and his team on the case. We think there's a lot of brand building we can do in these emerging markets. Zach do you have that piece on Apple we read? The one in Fast Company? Would you mind getting it?"

A few moments later, Zach reappeared and handed David the article, which had been neatly cut out and pasted to a sheet of cream cardboard.

"You see," said Laura excitedly, "when they were designing the packaging for the iPod Nano, they went through literally dozens of designs just to get the label right to show where you're meant to peel open the plastic packaging. Isn't that brilliant? Steve Jobs is such a perfectionist. He cares about every aspect of the Apple brand, which explains the company's success."

Well, thought David, stoking the emotion of consumers worldwide through inspired packaging may work well at Apple. But syringes in Central America?

Chapter 8

Valedictorians & MVPs

"Donna from HR is waiting for you," said Marjorie, as David arrived back at his office. She was winding the windows shut to keep out the hot, soupy air.

"You ever seen one of these?" he said, setting the tee down on Marjorie's desk. "It's an unbreakable golf tee. R&D came up with it."

He walked to his office where a woman around his own age was sitting on the chair facing his desk. She got up the moment he entered.

"Please, sit down. I'm David Hewitt. Thanks for coming to see me."

"Donna Archer. I'm the head of Human Resources."

"Great. So, tell me about them."

"About what?"

"Surgitec's human resources."

"Where would you like me to start? Two years ago, *Medical Supplier* magazine voted us the best place to work in the Midatlantic states, based on the complete package we offer to our employees—pay, pension, healthcare, vacation days. It was quite an honor."

"How did we do last year?"

"Another company won. But I've spoken to the editor, and I think we can regain the top spot this year."

"What do we have to do? Give everyone more time off?" Donna cocked her head, not appearing to get the joke.

"I'm just kidding," said David, as Donna plucked a file from a stack on her lap and passed it across the table.

EXECUTIVE
TEAM

Meet David and his Leadership Team
On-Line at www.smashing-silos.com

"I put together some numbers in preparation for your arrival. I think they provide a useful snapshot of our business." David opened it up. "Surgitec," read the headline. "Resourced for Wellness." He glanced down the bullet points. There were 847 employees here in Pennsylvania. Another 1,098 in two manufacturing plants in Puerto Rico and South Carolina. The rest were in the sales offices and distribution centers—a total of 2,419; 1,596 were men and 823 women. Eight percent of the workforce in Pennsylvania were classified as minorities. The employee churn rate was the lowest in the industry, though that was true across the board at Carson. Workforce stability was a company mantra, going back to its earliest days. Carson liked people to join the company and stay for their entire careers. The policy attracted a certain kind of worker: diligent, conservative, steadfast and loyal. The upside was that those were all wonderful qualities. Knowledge and talent rarely left the company. The downside was that it bred a kind of institutional complacency. People became deeply set in their ways.

"As you'll see, we have a good balance between the sexes," said Donna. "But we definitely need to do more work on diversity here in Harleysville."

"Any labor issues?"

"I'm proud to say that here in Pennsylvania, we have some of the best labor relations in corporate America. Last year, we had some trouble in Puerto Rico. Some activists tried to unionize the plant down there and we had to stop them. Other than that, though, George and I worked for many years to create a harmonious labor situation here at Surgitec, and I think we've achieved that. Our internal reviews show very high levels of employee satisfaction. We've increased the number of training sessions we offer, which certainly helps with employee morale. Every employee here in Harleysville now spends ten days a year in training and re-training, sharpening their existing skill sets and acquiring new ones. And for executives, every year there is a one-week training off-site, and every three years, they get to go to Carson University up in Rochester, New York, for three to six weeks. Then of course, all of our employees have access to the *i*University via the Carson portal, which offers business and language skills training to anyone who wants it. I feel confident in saying, David, that Surgitec is a leader when it comes to how we care for our people."

"That's great to hear. Tell me about performance. How do you review it?"

"Obviously, within each function, we work with managers to establish performance criteria, based on certain key factors."

"Such as?"

"Our most important tool is an annual three-hundred-sixty-degree review. Every employee receives feedback from those around them, and that's very important."

"How about financial targets?"

"Obviously, sales has its own system for how they measure and reward. Elsewhere, we try to limit the importance of purely financial goals and focus more on process rather than outcomes. Our philosophy is that if we can ace the process, the outcomes will take care of themselves." She nodded as she spoke, a trick David had been taught in a one-day body language seminar the company had sent him on. If you nod while you say something, you hope the other person will be lulled into agreeing with you, or at least imagine you are making sense.

"Surely outcomes are important."

"Yes, but our philosophy is that process is what we can control so that's where we focus." David watched her nodding and did not reply. She folded her hands on her stack of files. "Several years ago, you may recall, we had an unfortunate incident where a small group of employees were found to be selling some of our proprietary designs to a rival. These were men and women we had all worked with for years. It was very traumatic for the organization, David. Then four years ago, we were caught up in all that finger pointing about US companies that do their manufacturing overseas. Some of the big retailers and electronics manufacturers got the worst of it, but we were investigated by the International Labor Organization too. George had to go and do a town hall meeting with student activists at Penn State. It was a difficult few years. And then of course, you were at Carson throughout the SEC investigation, right?"

"Yes I was. "

"So you recall the fear that went around the company. You remember how they subpoenaed all those corporate files so they could figure out if we'd been backdating stock options for senior executives? Of course, it came to nothing. But afterward, George came to see me and he said the most important thing to Surgitec now was stability. Low churn. Employee satisfaction. The business needed time to take a deep breath and get back to normal. I think we're there now. The work force is aligned and there are no major stresses on our people. Thank heavens."

"And how did you get into this work?"

"I was an attorney. Hated it, like everyone does. A friend suggested HR, and I've never looked back."

"Could you do something for me, Donna?"

"Of course."

"I'm still meeting people here. But I'd like to see your files on my executive team. It'll help me a lot to understand them and your system of measuring and recording performance. Would that be OK?"

"I'll have the files to you this afternoon. No problem. And if you need any help understanding them, I'd be happy to walk you through them."

"Thank you."

They both turned to the door as they heard the sound of loud male voices, laughing and talking in the corridor outside. Marjorie appeared in the doorway.

"Sorry. The team from distribution is here to see you."

"I'm just finishing up here with Donna. I'll be with them in a couple of minutes." Marjorie disappeared back through the doorway. "Sorry. So, yes, if you could get me the reviews and then we can talk again. Also, I'd like to get a handle on those labor issues you mentioned. In case they ever crop up again, I'd like to familiarize myself with the situation."

"One final thing is this," said Donna, handing him a thick white envelope. "These are the forms you're required to fill out. I know you've done this with Carson, but these are Surgitec specific. It's confidentiality, as well as standard health and pensions stuff." David weighed the heavy stack of paper in his hand. "Everyone has to do it, I'm afraid. We're moving to an electronic system, which will make it quicker. But the sooner you can get through it, the sooner we can get you all set up."

David rose and walked her to the door. "Thanks for stopping by. We'll be speaking a lot more, I'm sure." As he opened the door and ushered Donna out, he saw four men standing beside Marjorie's desk, resembling the offensive line of a 1930s college football team—huge bodies stuffed into khaki Dockers and button downs, all topped by closely trimmed hair.

"Come on in guys," said David, waving them down toward him. They crammed down the hall and into David's office, making the large space feel suddenly small. David gestured to the sofas and the men sat down, the cushions sighing beneath their bulk. He sat down in a wooden armchair between the two sofas. "So, distribution. You're the guys who make it all happen." All four men laughed contentedly and nodded.

"Yes we do," said the largest of the four. "I'm Chuck Long, head of distribution, and this is Fred Davidson, who runs our truck fleet and handles air and rail freight, Arthur Stevens, who runs our distribution centers, and Lewis Atkins, who runs the technology back end for all of logistics. Combined, over a hundred years at Surgitec. A lot of experience."

"Good to know our products are in such seasoned hands."

"Yes, Sir. We're very proud of our work. We have the best, and I'm not boasting here, I think, but the best distribution system to hospitals, clinics, and medical offices of any company our size. We run everything from large trucks for delivering to hospitals, to small vans to serve small customers. It's a very broad range, but we own most of our vehicles, so that gives us a lot of flexibility."

"What's your biggest challenge?"

"What we try to avoid more than anything is stock-outs. We never want our customers to be without the products they need. We don't want a surgeon or a general practitioner ever running out of product. So we try to go above and beyond to provide the very highest level of customer service. We aim to "wow" the customer at every interaction. We know how hard the guys work to make and sell the product, so we want to do our piece to complete the transaction. If any one of us along this chain fails, we all fail, and we're conscious of that." Chuck leaned over the arm of his chair and tapped David on the knee. He could smell the lotion in Chuck's hair.

"Last week, we had this doctor's practice in Columbus, Ohio, that ran out of supplies. They called us on a Wednesday afternoon, around four forty p.m. Isn't that right guys? Our closest distribution center didn't have what they needed. But we had the supplies waiting for them when they got to the office on Thursday morning. We had one of our drivers drive eight hours from here, overnight, to make sure we got them their supplies. It's what makes our reputation."

"And on the cost side?"

"Our costs are spread among lots of customers and we do so much to keep them happy, that they're more than justified. You look at our on-time delivery record and our customer satisfaction levels and you'll see what our costs get us in terms of loyalty, which, when you're in our business, Mr. Hewitt, means a great deal."

"But which costs cause you the most anxiety?" The four men glanced at each other and as if by some form of telepathy nodded in agreement.

"Fuel," said Chuck. "Low, stable prices are good for us. The minute they start to rise or fluctuate, it makes it hard for us to plan and stay within budget. Fred was reading up on hedging, you know, using futures to cap our prices, but the guys up at corporate killed that before we even had a chance to try it out. So we do the best we can."

"Do you think I could spend a day with your guys one day? See how the distribution center works? Meet the drivers?" Chuck beamed with pleasure.

"It'd be our privilege. I think when you see our fleet and meet our guys, you'll be more than impressed."

"How about next Friday?"

Chuck looked around at his team. They shrugged and nodded.

"Friday would be good. You ever drive a truck, Mr. Hewitt."

"One summer back in college, I drove vans and light trucks for a moving company."

"Oh, you should see the rigs we've got. They're things of beauty. You can sleep in them, watch TV. They're like houses on wheels."

"Can't wait. I wish my son were here. He'd love them."

"Where is he?"

"France. We're in the process of moving back from France. I was working there for Carson."

"Ah, the French. Renault builds incredible trucks. They know what they're doing when it comes to trucks."

David got up and the four men followed suit, heaving themselves out of their low-slung seats with a flurry of audible wheezes.

"I'll see you next Friday."

At nine o'clock the following morning, David settled himself into one of the large leather seats at the head of the conference room table. The room was otherwise empty and the large screen at one end was blank. He pressed a button on the triangular intercom in front of him. "Ready when he is, Marjorie." There was a sudden crackle from the screen as it turned on.

The screen then flashed from gray to reveal Barry Johnson, resplendent in a lime green V-neck sweater and pink golf shirt, against a background of vivid gold wallpaper. "Coming at you live from Atlanta," boomed a voice through the speakers embedded in the ceiling. "Sorry I'm not up there this week, but the customers demand I play this tournament. Marjorie explained I hope. I'd have loved to show you 'round Harleysville. There's more than meets the eye. Thankfully. Hey, can we get this so I can see David," he said to someone off-screen. The image wobbled again. "There that's better. Now I can see you. How are you settling in? Your family joined you yet? Boy, they must hate you for dragging them away from Paris!"

"They'll be with me soon. We're sorting out the move. Thanks for sparing the time, Barry. When's your tee-time?"

"Oh, not for another hour. They're pretty civilized down here. Not like California, where they all like to be on the course by dawn and done by breakfast. Here it's more leisurely."

"Great. I'm jealous."

"Oh, don't be. It's just eighteen holes on a gorgeous course, followed by fat steaks and a lot of a boring sales talk. You aren't missing anything."

"I'm not sure I should believe you."

"Hah. You sound like my wife."

"I don't want to take up a lot of your time today, Barry. I can tell you're busy. But I did want to talk briefly, as I'm trying to meet everyone and didn't want you feeling left out."

"Very considerate of you, David."

"We'll go into everything in much greater detail when you get back, but I wanted to get your five minute version of how the business is doing. It'll help give me some perspective as I talk to all the other functions."

"Well, first of all, welcome to Surgitec, David. We were all just heart-broken to say goodbye to George, but he assured us we'd be in great hands with you. From a sales perspective, we're rocking it. You know, I've been in sales all my life, most of the time here with Surgitec, and I don't think we've ever been in this good shape. Our big accounts are rock solid and we've got a couple of new guys who are out there beating the bushes, going clinic to clinic, working the rural and suburban areas bringing in one new customer after another. So it's a combination of great, old relationships and new ones which are driving our volume."

"Any big issues I should know about?"

"I'm a straight talker, David. Everyone knows that about me. I don't sugar coat. It's not my style. My team would resent it and customers would hate it. I've always found truth to be the best policy. So I hope you'll understand. But there are two things holding me and my guys back. The first is price. We're out in the field every day fighting against competitors who undercut our prices by ten to fifteen percent, and sometimes twenty percent. We have to discount like crazy to get our product to move. Even then, it's hard to hold on to customers. You know, it's a damned near miracle we're still adding new accounts, sixty in the past eighteen months, with our prices as high as they are. If I were stepping into your shoes, I'd take a hard look at this because it makes our job a whole lot harder."

"And what's the second thing?"

"New products. We need more of them. What we have is starting to look pretty stale. R&D needs to come up with some new products and manufacturing needs to get them out of the door faster. Right now, we're selling products that customers can't get their hands on because manufacturing can't get them out of the plant on time. We need to synchronize this much better." As he said this, he interlocked his fingers. "We need better communication across the functions. If you could manage that, you'll see an instant improvement. Again, I'm giving this to you straight, David, because you're a Carson guy, and I know you like to work from facts and data. We're pulling in the customers. We've now got to figure out how to keep them, because the competition is changing. When we're out in the field, we're running into new companies all the time, run out of China or India, selling similar products for much less. We've got to sprint to stay ahead."

"Look, if you'd like, we can pick this up again this evening. I've got an hour between my round ending and dinner. But they're saying I need to get out to join my foursome. Was that helpful?"

"Very helpful. Thanks Barry. Look forward to meeting you in person."

The sound on the screen cut out, but David saw Barry pointing his finger at him and was sure he seemed to be saying, "You too, buddy."

Bob Grieve licked the mustard from his fingers and set down his three-inch high pastrami sandwich. It toppled all over his newspaper. He wiped his right hand quickly with a napkin and extended it to David. It was 4:30 in the afternoon.

"Excuse me. I just got in from the airport an hour ago. I needed some good American food after a week in San Juan."

"Carry on."

"Can I get you anything? Coke, Pepsi, Mountain Dew?"

"No, I'm good, thanks."

"Take a seat, then."

"Everything good in Puerto Rico?" asked David. "How often are you down there?"

"Once a month usually, but every two weeks at the moment. We've had to shut down a couple of assembly lines to retool them for new products."

"Do you speak Spanish?"

"My assistant down there calls it factory Spanish. I couldn't order lunch, but I can tell you how to say 'broken conveyor belt.' I should know more by now, but you know, you get comfortable communicating like you do and then you get lazy about getting better at it. You were in France, right?"

"I know exactly what you mean."

"So I hear you've been going around the company. Found out anything interesting?"

"Surgitec is a great company. Seems like there's tons of opportunity."

"Good. We need a fresh set of eyes."

"Why do you say that?"

"I've been in manufacturing for twenty-five years. I can tell you when processes get into a rut. We're in a rut here at Surgitec." He took another large bite of his sandwich. "Excuse me," he said with his mouth half full. "I can't help it when I have one of these things in front of me. My wife tells me they'll stop my heart in the end, but at least I'll go a happy man."

"Tell me more about this rut," prodded David.

"George was a great man. Don't get me wrong. We all loved him. Couldn't have had a nicer boss. But if you're in this business to improve things, which is why I got into it, it got a little frustrating. Provided we met some pretty modest targets, management was happy. There wasn't any cause to change."

"What did you want to change?"

"In manufacturing? Basically, it's poor planning. Sales and marketing keep multiplying the SKUs, adding products and packaging without taking a moment to think what it means for us. When we have to stop the line to adjust it to make a small batch of product for a small customer, it slows us right down. Then we can't get out enough of the bulk products on schedule, and then we've got even more customer complaints. Sales keeps making these promises to customers without even thinking about manufacturing. And R&D doesn't bother to consult us before trying to introduce their cockamamie ideas."

"Anything else."

"You heard about the new ERP system?"

"Finance tells me it's great."

"Course they would. For them, it's just bits and bytes. When we first went live with it, all our production in Puerto Rico just stopped because the orders were all wrong. Then our inventory systems crashed. We're still recovering from that. Customers will ask for a product and we know we've made it, and we've certainly paid for it, we just can't find it, and the system doesn't help us, so we end up on these wild goose chases through our own factories, warehouses, and distribution hubs. Then I'm having to pay overtime, so my costs keep going up, which I then have to justify at the monthly meetings. So I get a hard time from finance, when it's their damn system that's causing me grief."

"Donna in Human Resource mentioned some labor problems in Puerto Rico, but said they were all now resolved."

"In her dreams."

"What do you mean?"

"The agitators are still there. The unions are strong down there and they've got us in a lock. Especially after all the bad publicity around American companies that outsource manufacturing. They know that the moment we play hardball, they can bring down every journalist in the region to write about the battle between the poor, Puerto Rican laborers and the evil gringo corporation."

"How do you deal with it?"

"For now, we've pretty much given into their demands. But we're also looking for alternatives. Costa Rica might work. Or maybe even move everything to Asia. That seems to be where the whole world is moving."

"What's going to help you with the decision?"

"Cost. Labor relations. Transport issues. There's no magic bullet here. All I need is time to manage through the issues."

"We could all use time, couldn't we? Maybe I'll have that Coke."

Bob reached down to a small refrigerator and pulled one out and passed it over. "Do you need a glass?"

"No, this is fine." David cracked it open. "Tell me Bob, do you think there's growth in this business?" Bob smiled at him and wiped his fingers again on what was left of fast dissolving napkin.

"You mean revenue or margin growth?"

"Let's talk about both."

"Revenue, sure. Sales are always bragging about that. You can grow Surgitec in the US and overseas. Emerging markets are going to need the kind of stuff we make. They'll probably have plants that just do knock-offs of our best-sellers, but we can still compete."

"And margin?"

"Take a look around. This is not a tightly run ship. You've got money leaking out all over the place."

"What have you done to stop it?"

"We run our factories on a shoestring. We keep our wages low and I do my best with our materials costs. Where it all goes wrong is when we're constantly juggling to accommodate more SKUs. The labor issues are what they are. You'll have them wherever you go. It's the internal stuff that drives me crazy."

"What would you do if you were in my shoes?" asked David.

"Simplify the product line. Get our ERP system to work."

"Simplify the product line at the expense of revenue? Sales is telling me they want more products."

"Well, you'd have to persuade sales. They'll always want more in their bag so they don't have to convince people to value what we've already got."

"You ever read about Jack Welch at General Electric? He said that every business unit in the company had to be either number one or two in its market. If not, they would be sold. Do you think Surgitec meets that test?"

"Some years yes, others no," said Bob.

David drank down the last of his Coke.

"You enjoy the rest of that," said David pointing down to Bob's nearly finished sandwich. "I'm going to think about what you said. Thanks for being so straightforward with me. It saves a lot of time."

"My pleasure." As he was turning to leave, he noticed a photograph of an older man holding up a large trout.

"Who's that?"

"My old man."

"Where did he fish?"

"Lake Huron. We lived in Detroit."

"No kidding. Me too. We used to fish Lake St. Claire. What did your dad do out there?"

"Machine worker for auto parts. Union guy. Lifer. Worked and got out while the going was still good out there. Got a great pension, thanks to the UAW."

"You ever go back there," asked David.

"Once a year. My mother's in a home out there. Most of my friends have left. They're all over the place now. You?"

"My father died a few months ago. I'll go out next month to see my mother. But you're right, everyone seems to have left."

"Story of American manufacturing right there," commented Bob.

"I'll see you on Tuesday afternoon."

"Sure. At the executive team meeting. See you then. You've probably got a lot to think about."

David sat down wearily on the sofa in his hotel room in downtown Philadelphia. On the coffee table in front of him was a stack of files Marjorie had given him to read over the weekend. What time is it in Paris, he wondered—1:00 a.m. Much too late to call.

He flicked on the television. ESPN SportsCenter burbled away with reports on games and athletes, which no longer interested him. It was remarkable how quickly sports moved on when you left the country for a little while. One day, he would be re-immersed. But not now. The cable news channels were taken up by angry men and women bellowing at each other or into the camera. Where did all this anger come from? He turned it off, went over to the refrigerator, and pulled out a beer. He opened a drawer and took out a packet of nuts. "Luxury Mix," said the label. He checked the price. $5. The CFO's pudgy face flashed before his eyes. He opened them anyway. Nuts were nuts, he decided, luxury or not.

The top file had come from HR. It contained the performance appraisals for the executive team. He leafed through them, one by one. "Outstanding," "excellent," "great team player," the superlatives cascaded off the page. Every manager at Surgitec, it seemed, was a combination valedictorian and MVP. Laura Chan was described as "terrific with staff and sensitive to people of diverse backgrounds." Andy in finance was "decisive, fair, and punctual." That last one was what you said when you had nothing else to say. But still, hardly a negative. Bob Grieve was a "great manager and ambassador for the business, fully deserving of his five star rating." Chuck in distribution was a "disciplined manager who maintained high staff morale" while Barry Johnson had "successfully led Surgitec's expansion into exciting new markets, far exceeding plan."

The extraordinary thing was that not one of these reports mentioned the company's financial performance. It was as if all these people were performing for each other's benefit and that somehow the actual business of Surgitec would take care of itself. What kind of plan was it that Barry Johnson had exceeded if net income from Surgitec remained flat? Why were they all patting themselves so vigorously on the back when the numbers were so anemic? They were all clearly good people, intelligent, hard-working employees. But somehow, they were not all pulling together to achieve the returns that Carson expected.

David began to take notes. On Monday morning, he had to go to Carson's HQ for the monthly meeting of business unit heads. It was far earlier than he would have wanted, but the calendar was not built around him. After just ten days in the job, he couldn't imagine they'd give him a hard time.

Chapter 9

I'm Getting You Help

"You're saying that R&D costs are twenty-five percent over where they should be? That's just not acceptable." Elliot Davis drilled his finger into the table, raising his voice as he spoke. "Who's taking responsibility for this?"

"They say they have a lot of great products in the pipeline…"

"It's not they anymore, David. It's you. You're running Surgitec now," Elliott snarled.

"We're going to sort through the products in development and see what we have. Obviously, with costs at this level, we're going to be cutting some programs and scaling back others."

"You mentioned labor issues in Puerto Rico. George told us last month that these were fully resolved. And now you're telling us they're back."

"I just don't think they were as resolved as we thought," explained David, as Elliot slapped the table and turned away in disgust. "There aren't any problems right now, but I wanted to warn you in advance that there could be more trouble in the coming months. The problem has not gone away for good."

"And marketing? They're fifteen percent over budget. What's going on there?"

"They've invested in several new product launches in Latin America. We should claw back this money in the next few months."

"It would be the first time in recorded history anyone has clawed back money from marketing," cracked Elliott.

Linda sat back in her chair, watching the argument further down the table.

"I think it's high time we got rid of Surgitec," said Elliot. "It really has no place in the Carson portfolio. Its return on capital is in the tank compared to our other businesses. Its cost management is subpar, and despite marketing's expensive efforts, it doesn't appear to be dramatically growing revenue. Linda?"

Linda said nothing, but looked at David.

"That would be premature," said David. "Surgitec has been a great business for Carson over the years. And it can be a great business again."

"Are you putting yourself on the line here, David?" said Elliot.

"Yes, I am."

"What makes you think you can turn it around?"

"I think there are good people at Surgitec and some great products. Our customers seem loyal and with a little more discipline—"

"You think no one tried any discipline while you were in France, David?" said Elliot. "What do you think we were all doing here? Firing spitballs and chewing gum as if the teacher had left the classroom? There has been no lack of discipline at Surgitec."

David wanted to respond in kind, but he held his tongue.

"I think we can improve ROCE to at least Carson-wide levels within a year to eighteen months."

"Hah!" exclaimed Elliot. "Where are you now? Four and a half percent? And you anticipate getting returns up to twenty percent in eighteen months? Go knock yourself out. How do plan to do that, David?"

"Give me a few more weeks and I'll have a plan for you."

"I think that's fair," interjected Linda. "Let's move on."

"Enjoy yourself back there?" said Linda. They were sitting in her office. After the meeting had ended, Elliot had brushed rudely past David.

"It's not what I expected."

"Elliot wanted his own man in that job. You should know that. Not that it makes any difference to what you do now that you have it. So what are you going to do?" Linda took a sip of coffee from a paper cup. "You must have had a chance to kick the tires by now."

"I should never have committed myself to that target. Increase ROCE four-fold in eighteen months. What was I thinking?"

"Welcome home, David. You were thinking exactly the right thing. That you weren't going to be pushed around by Elliot and that you would like to prove him wrong. Now all you have to do is make it happen."

"What would you do?"

"Wrong question. Not my business. It's your business not mine. Don't get me wrong, I want you to succeed. But you have to own this change. Not me. I'll support you if I think you're doing a good job, but really, you're on your own. That's what running a business is all about."

"I'm just not sure we have the internal capabilities to do this."

"To figure out the problems, you mean?"

"Yes. I read the performance reviews, and everyone's supposedly doing great. And then I look at financial performance, and it's just stuck. Sales blames R&D and manufacturing, manufacturing blames sales and marketing, finance thinks the answer is in staying in cheap hotels and printing on both sides of the paper…" Linda burst out laughing.

"Tell me something new, David. You know, it's always like this. Everyone is covering their own rear. That's corporate life."

"So how do you get them motivated to change? I can tell them the company's going to be sold, but they don't believe it. They all think Surgitec is like Carson's darling son; that it will never be sold whatever it does."

"Now you know why CEOs get paid. This is everyday stuff."

"I feel like I might need an outsider's view. To validate what it is we need to do. If I try to do things from the inside, it looks like I'm trashing my own company. I can feel the resistance even before it's organized."

"Bring in the consultants, you mean, to make the tough decisions for you?"

"That's not what I meant."

"Yes it is. Hold on." She pressed his intercom. "Ellen, could you bring in the strategic consulting reports on Surgitec?"

"You commissioned a review of Surgitec's strategy?"

"We went through this with George. He was too close to the company. So the previous CEO wanted some fresh eyes on the problem. We hired two of the top tier strategy firms, one after another, to go in and take a look. Ah, thank you Ellen. Here's what they came up with." She dumped a large stack of bound PowerPoint decks on the table. The first set was titled *New Horizons*. The second was called *Surging Into the Future: Surgitec's Tomorrow*. "Go on, take a look." Linda turned her attention to her Blackberry while David picked up *New*

Horizons.

"The world's population is growing," it began. "More people means more demand for medical supplies. Surgitec's opportunity lies wherever human beings are in need of treatment." It was downhill from this windy beginning. Several charts indicated what Surgitec's revenue would look like if it expanded its focus on emerging markets beyond its current footprint in Latin America. But this would require enormous changes at the company.

Surging Into the Future was the same. It began with a graphic showing the silhouette of a runner bursting through a finishing tape. The report was full of charts from the World Health Organization describing the number of hospital visits per capita in different parts of the world. It was tangential at best, irrelevant at worst. The report concluded: "Enormous possibility lies ahead for Surgitec. But it demands dramatic change. A new sense of strategic direction is required." Perfect, thought David. It sounded grand and looked impressive, but it said nothing. He closed the final volume and slumped back into his seat.

"What did you think?" said Linda, without looking up from her Blackberry.

"I doesn't look like George's heart was in it," surmised David. "These studies are always as much a reflection of the customer's input as the consultants.' If this is all they could come up with, he couldn't have been giving them much to work with."

"Exactly what I thought. There's some interesting stuff there. Good theory. The key trends on the global health industry, the emerging markets stuff, but there's nothing that is going to add a dollar to our bottom line this year or next."

"I don't think the basic problem is strategic," said David. "And on a department by department basis, the operations are in good shape as well. The problems are the lack of focus on the overall business, and on its profitability. Everyone needs to get out of their silos and work on making money."

"You know, I think there are a lot of people at Carson who couldn't calculate operating income if their lives depended on it. It's not their fault. It's the same at a lot of big companies," said. Linda. She set down her phone and looked intently at David. "In a small business, cash is what matters. It's what you measure. In big corporations, there's always a chest of cash you can dip into. So you stop worrying about it. You can lose money and people say it's just a loss, as if it's just a number on an income statement and no one has to pay for it. We get so fat and happy in these big corporations that we have the luxury of fretting over team building and diversity training and all the other massive time-sinks. The problem is, David, it's dull working like this, isn't it? People like you and me, we want to see strong profits and returns on capital. We don't just want to see our employees performing well-drilled processes like a bunch of retirees doing Tai Chi in a park. We want results."

"That's why I became a general manager."

"So back to the question Elliot asked you. What are you going to do about Surgitec?"

"Improve its profitability. But where do I begin? What do I need to know to even figure out how to start? It's like holding a bunch of tangled string. You can try to pick it apart gently, but that takes forever, or you can hack through it with scissors, which in a company like Carson is impossible. Now we have these ROCE targets Elliot is pressing me on and I'm wondering how to get from here to there."

"When's your wife arriving?"

"Not for another few weeks. There's a lot to sort out and she's enjoying her last summer in France."

"So you have the chance to really focus on this. Listen, I hear you, David. It's a slow growth, price conscious market. You've got doubts about your team, even though they've all got top ratings. You've got a stretch objective that would shell-shock your team if you shared it with them. The ERP implementation has been a disaster, your costs are out of line, you need a four hundred percent increase in earnings, and your family is three thousand miles away. Welcome to my world. But I'm telling you that I believe this can be done, with a bit of willpower, intellect, and charm. We can turn Surgitec back into a high performing business, get it back to being the darling of the corporation like it was in the seventies and eighties. But you're going to need help. Maybe you could do this on your own, but not on the schedule you promised the executive committee." Linda picked up the telephone and dialed.

"Ed, Linda Thomas here. Doing good thanks, how about you?" Linda nodded and smiled as they exchanged pleasantries. "Listen, I've got one of my business unit heads here. Could really use your help. You have any time?" She paused and listened. "That sounds great. See you soon, Ed." She set the phone down again and scribbled a number on a notepad.

"Who is he?"

"A consultant, but not the kind who writes *New Horizons*. Consider him your special agent, and let him dig around the numbers."

"And you've arranged for me to meet him?"

"Yes. He's going to give you a call. You want greater profitability, and his thing is greater profitability. Expanding the operating margins."

"How does he do it?"

"Don't ask too many questions now. Just show up tomorrow and you'll find out."

"Who is this guy?"

"He helped me a lot in my last business unit. In fact, I'd say his work got me this job."

"But you're not going to tell me anything else?"

"Trust me. I'm getting you help."

Like what, though, wondered David?

Help? Or a parachute?

Chapter 10

Mining A Sea Of Data

David arrived early at work the next morning.

"Good morning," said Ernie cheerfully. "How are you liking being back in Pennsylvania, Mr. Hewitt? You see how the Phillies are doing? World Series, I reckon."

"Good morning, Ernie. Dream on." He spun through the turnstile and took the elevator up to his office. The evening before, he had asked Marjorie to pull together any internal reports prepared over the past eighteen months addressing the issue of performance improvement. A slim pile now waited for him on his desk. He went and made himself a cup of coffee and sat down. It was 6:00 am. He would have three hours to himself.

He began sifting through the reports. The first two were similar to the strategic review documents, packed with lurid but vacuous graphics, proposing changes that would take years to implement and required a huge capital investment. A few more were highly specific and technical. Manufacturing saw an opportunity in using more performance control technologies to control variance in its production lines. Distribution was proposing another hedging strategy to manage the volatility of fuel prices. Nothing too radical.

The final document was a set of ten pages stapled together. The cover read *Surgitec: Opportunities*. It was dated two months ago. He flicked onto the first page. The first line read: "Surgitec's market share is less than desirable for the amount of brand exposure the company receives. Costs are excessive and there

TRANSFORMATION PROCESS

Review Ed's Transformation Process On-Line at www.smashing-silos.com

is little or no understanding of the sources of the company's profitability." David rocked back in his chair, took a long sip of coffee and reached for a red pen on his desk. He looked back to the cover to see the name of the author: 'Alice Miles, Manager, Financial Planning and Analysis.' Hmm, never heard of her.

The document began by comparing Surgitec's financial metrics to its key rivals. Not only was Surgitec not meeting Carson's expectations, but its expense levels and returns were far below the industry averages as well. Next, the report detailed where Surgitec's revenues were going—big discounts and oversized COGS and OPEX. On the third page, she had done an analysis that stopped David short.

She had ranked every one of Surgitec's customers by revenue and then categorized by size them into A, B and C segments. She had then prepared a chart, a Pareto, which revealed that just 18 percent of Surgitec's customers produced 80 percent of its revenue.

Just as bad, the company's product portfolio seemed to be skewed as well, with 80 percent of the sales coming from just 14 percent of the products. The graphs posed the startling question that had been struggling to form in David's mind since he arrived: why was Surgitec wasting so much time and so many resources on customers and products who produced little revenue and probably even less profit?

He went straight to the HR directory to find Alice's file. She was twenty-seven years old. Graduated from Penn State in business and accounting. Had worked for PWC for two years as a trainee before coming to Surgitec two years ago. She reported directly to Andy Butler, the CFO.

He opened up an email and addressed it to Alice and Andy: "Just read Alice's report on Surgitec's financial opportunities. I'd like you to come and present it to me. Please call Marjorie to arrange a time this week. Thanks, David." He then sent an email just to Andy: "Your department has done some great work here. Looking forward to talking with you about it as soon as possible."

At 7:36 a.m., David's telephone rang. Marjorie wasn't in yet. The only other person with his private line was Maria, but she always called on his cell. He picked it up.

"David Hewitt?" said the voice on the other end.

"Yes."

"Ed Chase, here. Linda Thomas asked me to give you a call."

"Yes, of course. Linda tells me that you're the guy to help me turn around Surgitec."

"We'll see about that, but I appreciate the vote of confidence. Do you have some time to meet today?"

"Let me see, today is kind of backed up—"

"I can be in Harleysville in an hour if that works. I have a flight out of Philadelphia this afternoon. I'm heading to Tokyo for the next week."

"OK then, I guess it'll have to be this morning. Sure, let's get together in an hour. You know how to get here?"

"Don't worry about me. I'll see you then."

With a consultant invited in by the CEO now en route, the reality of making big changes at Surgitec started to weigh on David with a new level of gravity, and a new sense of urgency. He felt an overwhelming urge to speak to Maria, and impulsively dialed her cell. She answered. In the background, he could hear the burble of department store muzak.

"Where are you?" he asked.

"We're in Le Bon Marche." David could see the Left Bank store now, the Metro stop at Sevres-Babylone and the chic French couples strolling outside in the late summer sunshine after a lazy lunch. "The kids are getting a last go at the toy store. You remember, the one in the basement."

"Of course I remember. With the puppets and the three hundred dollar baby outfits."

"And the wooden toys you loved." He recalled the wooden boats and cars, throwbacks to a childhood even before his own.

"How is everything?"

"We're having a great time, David. Somehow, the prospect of leaving is making me do all the things we thought about but never did. We went up to Montmartre yesterday, got drawings of the boys by one of those cheesy street artists. I think we're going to try out the catacombs tomorrow. Hope they're not too scary. How's Harleysville?"

"Oh, you know. The giant Toys 'R' Us next to the Friendly's isn't exactly the Left Bank."

"I've been looking at houses online. Trying to find one near Germantown, for the Friends School. I think we should try and find one of those old Dutch houses, with the thick stone walls and slate roofs."

"And the low ceilings and bad plumbing."

"You're not putting me in some contractor special, David. You do realize that?"

"And you're not putting me in an episode of Antiques Roadshow." He heard her laugh, three thousand miles away.

"Four more weeks, then. We're going up to Brittany to stay with Louise and her family. They've got a house on the coast."

"God, I'm envious."

"You could never stand to hang out with Louise and Roger."

"You're right. But somehow they seem better in hindsight."

"Doesn't everything?"

"How are the boys?"

"Really well. I'm spoiling them. They get chocolate crepes most days after the playground. I want to overwhelm them with Frenchness before we come home. Then hope some of it sticks. Probably won't, but it's worth a try."

"Send them my love. Let's talk tomorrow."

"Try me before noon if you can."

"So five thirty in the morning my time? You really care about my sleep."

"I'll speak to you then."

David rested his head in his hands for a moment after hanging up his phone. Just four more weeks without family obligations. He had to make the most of his time.

David walked back from the restroom to his office to find an elegant-looking man in a dove gray suit and open-necked white shirt sitting at his meeting table. The man rose and offered his hand.

"David Hewitt. I'm guessing." His face was worn and brown, his grey hair swept back. He looked as if he had just stepped off a beach on the Shore.

"And you must be Ed Chase."

"Correct. Linda told me this used to be George's office. Charming man, George."

"That's what everyone tells me."

"You haven't met him?"

"Once he left here, he set off on a three-month tour of golf courses in the western states. All he left me was a welcome letter."

"Do you have it?"

"Sure." David walked to his desk and pulled it out of the middle drawer where he had found it. Ed put on a pair of reading glasses and began to read. He chuckled all the way through.

"Very George," he said.

"What do you mean?"

"Very attentive to people's needs. But tell me, Linda asked me to come in and talk to you, to see if there's any way I can help. Let's sit down."

David pulled out a chair.

"As I said to Linda, and I guess this is all just between the three of us, we have five issues here. The first is the people. They've grown up in a very comfortable period for Surgitec and I'm not sure they understand the urgent need for the company to change. The second is the lousy market we're in, we're being squeezed by low-cost competitors, every day another company pops up in Asia making the same stuff for less—"

"Hold it right there. You're going too fast. Tell me about yourself, David. Where you grew up, what you've been doing that brought you here."

"OK. I grew up in Detroit. My dad was a machinist, my mother a stay-at-home mom. Went to college at Notre Dame."

"You a football fan?"

"Of course. What else is there to do in South Bend? I was the assistant manager of the team. Helped the coaching staff with some projects, did travel arrangements. Also played a lot of basketball."

"Then afterward?"

"I joined Carson as part of its graduate trainee program and have been with the company ever since; spent most of my twenties rotating through functions, gaining experience. Then I worked in baby care products for a few years, which is where I worked for Linda. Spent some time running distribution in Eastern Europe, then back here in Philadelphia in sales, then finance at corporate for five years, before being sent to Europe to be the country manager for France."

"So, you're Carson through and through."

"I guess you could say that."

"Have you ever been in a turnaround situation?"

"Not until now. Well, the Eastern European distribution center was a mess before I got there. But the business was a virtual monopoly, so we could afford to make some mistakes, which was fortunate, because we made a lot of them."

"So you have experience in manufacturing, sales, and finance?"

"And I did some marketing for baby-care."

"Very good. So you understand how all these different functions mesh."

"Sure."

"So why do you seem so surprised by what you've found here?"

"Well, I guess, it's my responsibility now…"

"To make sales and marketing get along? To get manufacturing to love sales? These are the great intractable problems of business, David. You hear it everywhere. Sales suspects marketing doesn't do enough to support them. Manufacturing blames R&D for coming up with products that are too hard to make. It's no different from a football team. When things go wrong, the receivers blame the quarterbacks, who blames the offensive line, who say if only the defense did their job."

"But I'm sure you've got a remedy. So what do you suggest I do?"

"Don't get ahead of yourself. First you have to diagnose the problem. Is it really just poor coordination amongst the functions that's causing Surgitec's problems? What else could it be?"

"I'm trying to figure that out." He got up and walked to his desk. "I came across this report this morning. It was the first thing I've read that intrigued me." He passed it to Ed. "It argues that we've got a lot of customers who contribute very little to our financial performance, besides adding costs." Ed glanced through it.

"Do you agree?"

"I wish I knew enough to corroborate it. I haven't found this kind of analytical work in any of the other reports I've read. The numbers I see are all top level roll-ups without much detail. It's hard to get any clarity."

"It's hard but it's not impossible," said Ed. "You just have to look in the right places and demand it. Tell me, David, how many customers does Surgitec have?"

"Fifteen hundred, two thousand. Around that."

"And how many SKUs?"

"Oh, thousands. Manufacturing was complaining to me about that."

"You should know the answer to both of those questions off the top of your head." David clicked and un-clicked the pen he was holding in his right hand.

"I'll get them for you."

"That's not the point," said Ed. "The point is that you've been here for what, two and a half, three weeks, and no one has bothered to give you these facts, because no one thinks they're important."

"They've given me lots of other facts," said David.

"Of course. They give you the facts that show themselves in the best possible light. The quotas they have met, the awards they have won, the targets achieved. But none of that means anything to you if the larger goal of improved profitability is not achieved. Correct?"

"Sure," agreed David.

"So you need to find your own facts. The ones that reveal the true levers of control. Because right now, you're limited not because you don't know which dials to turn and buttons to push, but because you haven't even found the dashboard. People always want to lead you off to admire the view from where they're sitting, because they can't bear to look at the iceberg looming up ahead. It's your job as the head of this business unit to navigate past the iceberg even while everyone else is looking at the sunset."

David stared down at the table.

"I'm going to make a guess, David. But it's an educated one, because I've seen companies like Surgitec before. Solid, foundation businesses on the surface. But scratch away and you find a lot of unnecessary moving parts. I'm guessing that the problem here is a lot of complexity in your product line, in your customer service functions, and your internal support functions. All that complexity is taking a toll on your cost structure and if you don't manage it, it's going to manage you."

"So what do you propose? A product review?"

"We're going to start by working the numbers in much more detail than you ever thought possible."

"You're going to have to fish them out of the ERP first."

"That's not a problem. Did that in Linda's last business, before she became CEO."

"What do you need?"

"It's more like, 'who have you got?' Who here really knows the systems and the numbers?"

"So we need a team, huh? We could start with the woman who wrote this report."

"Great. I'll need two to three people who are good with data, have access to your systems, and know the business."

"What else?"

"I'll need a place to set up a war room, some place with a lot of wall space to post our analysis."

"And what are you going to do?"

"We're going to go through your business customer by customer, transaction by transaction, and figure out where you're making money, and where you're losing it."

"Transaction by transaction? Isn't that a little extreme for an $1.2 billion business?" asked David.

"Unconventional, perhaps, but not extreme. We need to get right down to the invoice line item level and re-build your financials from the bottom up."

"My CFO tells me our financials are in great shape already. We cleared our corporate audit, no problem. And we just spent millions updating our ERP system. I don't have a lot of time to make an impact here, Ed. Starting with a big administrative project, like re-building the financials from the invoice line item level on up, sounds like a lot of extra work."

"I understand. Surgitec has invested a lot in its ERP systems. But this modeling effort is the foundation for the entire process. An ERP system is only as good as you demand it to be. Getting this profitability model right is the key to getting your organization focused on profitability and away from their departmental pet projects. You know the people aren't the problem here. What they're lacking is the right guideposts."

"What's wrong with using the financial statements we have to establish the right guideposts?" asked David.

"OK. Let's go a little deeper. Who are the corporate financial statements for? Are they meant for employees, or even managers?"

"I guess not."

"Right. They're for shareholders, creditors, analysts on Wall Street, the owners of the business, the CEO, people whose job it is to look from the top down. What interests them is overall profitability. They want a quick snapshot. All the grainy details that get rolled up into the P&L are of little interest to them," said Ed

"OK, I'm following your logic."

"So when your Finance Department closes your books, they're allocating revenues and expenses in buckets that matter to the readers of the financial statements. They'll split up results by major product categories or regions, but that's it. The accounting rules don't require them to do anything more than that."

"So why don't we just do a better job communicating our product line and regional results, the details one level down from the financial statements, more broadly? Can't we just do that and train the rank-and file to make better use of the data we already have?"

"You could," said Ed. "But let's think about what's really at issue here. It isn't just communication. It's control and action. How can you use the data inside the company to manage the business on a day-to-day basis? How can you use it to set the right incentives and measure the right outcomes? You see, when a front line employee or middle manager sees a line item on a financial statement like 'selling expense' or 'cost of goods sold,' do you think they feel empowered to do anything about it, especially if it's hundreds of millions of dollars? It's not that they don't care. It's just that their day-to-day actions seem so immaterial in relation to those big numbers that they feel they can't control them. So instead, they focus on what they can control. They get their deliveries out on time. They sign up new customers. They come up with new products. And they honestly believe they're making money."

"Well, you're right, those objectives are precisely what's showing up in everyone's review. But those are hardly bad things to focus on. If we didn't focus on execution, the business would grind to a halt," said David.

"True enough," agreed Ed. "But what's Alice's report telling us? That all those new products and new customers aren't contributing as much revenue as they should. Even if everyone individually is doing his or her best, the company's performance is still lackluster. But here's what's exciting. What do you think could happen if all the effort that went into meeting particular functional targets - expedited shipments, new product launches, customer acquisition, whatever it happens to be, all the things which make your employees justifiably proud - went instead to ensuring that each and every customer was profitable?

"I've no doubt they could do it. We've got a good team here and everyone really cares about the company," said David.

"So why aren't they focused on making money?" prodded Ed. "It's because no one is telling them that customer profitability is their responsibility. They assume someone else is worrying about it. If you want them to focus on profitability, you need to establish profitability as the organization's top strategic imperative. Every employee here needs to keep that idea on the top of their minds. That's how you build profitability into your culture."

"You know, I didn't see profitability mentioned anywhere on anyone's review. It's not even a performance metric for the department heads."

"That's the reality of where you're at today, so you need to step up and establish the imperative for profitability. If your reward and recognition programs don't focus on profitability, you shouldn't be surprised when your profitability falls short. Get your team on board, and paint it on the front of the building, if you have to. Then use the data we develop to guide your people as they go. They need to be able to link every one of their actions today with the goal of profitability in the future. They need to be able to see the relevant issues, have the means to address them, and know that they are being held accountable for getting them resolved. Let me lay it out for you." Ed stepped up to a whiteboard on the wall of David's office and began sketching and writing quickly. After a couple of minutes, he stepped back to let David see what he had written.

Model Your Profitability ⟩ Realign the Business ⟩ Empower the Organization

Commit to the Business Case   Establish your Strategic Imperatives

"This is how it all fits together. It's not about just one thing. It's about getting the right data, making the right top-level decisions, and then empowering the organization so that they can make the right decisions at their level into the future. Despite all the fancy charts we'll be generating, there's really no spreadsheet magic here. This only works if you can make the tough decisions based on the right information and persuade others to do the same. It's on you as the leader, David."

"So it seems you've got the motivational speaker part of the job down pat, but before we start that mural on the front of my headquarters, why don't you take me through that process you described in a bit more detail," panned David.

"OK, let's talk through it," agreed Ed. "As I mentioned, developing a granular, actionable view of your profitability is the first step. Not only will this work guide our decision-making, but it will also give you the kind of hard hitting financial information you need to get your team committed to changing their ways. They're going to see in plain black-and-white numbers just how many customers, products, industry segments, distribution centers, and territories are losing money. For an executive, there's simply no way you can ignore that type of data."

"Once we have a validated profitability model and start to derive some of the important insights, it's time for you to start selling," continued Ed. "We'll use the model to come up with a precise plan on how we'll get to your corporate objectives, and craft that into a business case that you can present to the executive committee at Carson. You'll need to put a stake in the ground to signal the kind of performance that Surgitec is capable of delivering."

"But more importantly," elaborated Ed, "we'll need to figure who from your internal Surgitec team is on board, and who's going to fight you along the way. The best way to do that is to collaborate on setting the strategic imperatives for business. Strategic imperatives aren't intricate strategies or tactics. They're simple guiding principles that you use to run the business, and that you can easily communicate across the organization. We'll arrive at these collaboratively as we work through the process, but it seems Linda has already been quite clear in establishing the first one." Ed paused as he jotted the first imperative on the white board.

Strategic Imperative #1:
Achieve a 20% Return on Capital Employed

He continued, "Your imperatives will be hierarchical—so achieving your required return should come first—and they also need to be quantifiable whenever possible. As a second example, most of my clients agree that customer relationships must be profitable. If your team won't come together on those types of imperatives, you might not have the right team."

"So the profitability data that we're going to develop will be the basis for our pitch to the executive committee, to my own team, and the broader Surgitec organization," paraphrased David. "The selling and the communication process will be important, both up and down the organization. I understand why we'll need defensible data to get everyone on board."

"That's right, and once you've done that, the real work begins. First we'll need a design for how the organization is going to function, then we'll need to implement all the changes necessary to implement that design. This will likely mean adjustments to prices, discounts, product offerings, distribution arrangements, service policies, and even our internal support groups. There will be some tough conversations, but when you're done you'll have the business honed on its most profitable areas."

"Where does it go from there? Do we live happily ever after?" teased David.

"The final phase is actually the most important," continued Ed, "because it's going to enable the business to keep making improvements into the future. We're going to arm your sales people, your product managers, your distribution team, and even your plant managers with detailed profitability reports. We're going to ask them to carefully plan out their business performance, and then review the results with them every month. When unfavorable variances spring up, they'll be accountable—and empowered—to go fix them. This approach will make sure that you're not facing these same performance issues in future periods, and will enable you to monitor the effectiveness of your front line contributors. Needless to say, if you're losing money at that level, you're not going to make it up later."

"OK, I get it," surrendered David. "We can start with the financial modeling and assessment work and see what it tells us. When can you start?"

"Two weeks, when I'm back from Japan. If you can give me a conference room and a few capable people, we can get right to it," said Ed.

"Let's give it a try. See you two weeks from today, that would be Monday the twenty-third, nine a.m."

"Make it eight. Best to get a jump on the rest of the company."

"I think that must be the fastest consulting hire in history," joked David.

"It was clearly meant to be. But, I do need to know one more thing. Why?"

"What do you mean?"

"Very simple question. Why bother? You're a Carson man. You've come this far. Carson will probably take care of you for the rest of your life if you decide to keep your head down. Why take the risk?"

"You think trying to improve Surgitec is a risk?"

"Of course."

"But isn't that my job?"

"Come on, David. You're not so naïve. If you want to change a place like this, you're going to create fear and anxiety, you're going to upset people. If you really want to go through all that, I need to understand your motivation."

David was silent for a minute. Ed kept his gaze fixed on him.

"It's why we do this, isn't it? To build better businesses. To make them sustainable. To give them a future."

"But you, David. Why you? Let me put it like this. When I first worked with Linda, she was in charge of a struggling business unit. It was in worse shape than Surgitec. And I told her then that the only way to improve it was by creating transparency and accountability. Now those are more than just corporate buzzwords. What they mean in practice is a readiness to face and tell the truth.

So the question is this, are you ready to be the leader who tells Surgitec the truth? Do you care enough to tell Surgitec the truth? If you do, it will be ugly for a while. Ideally, you get up on your soapbox, make your pitch, lay out the strategic imperatives, and everyone cheers and carries you on their shoulders to victory. But the reality is that you won't win everyone over. There'll be push-back and hostility. Some people will probably leave. Good people. And even then there is no guarantee of success.

"On the other hand," he continued, "if you decide to just carry on with business as usual, you can probably ride this career of yours to a quiet retirement, with much less risk. Your wife will be happy, your kids secure, your pension all locked up. This isn't just about doing a job, David. You've got a lot at stake here. I'm telling you this, because now is a good time to say 'no.'"

David said nothing.

"Think about it, then." Ed got up and walked toward the door. "You have my numbers."

Just as he was closing the door, David rose from his seat.

"Yes. Fine."

"Fine what?"

"Let's go find the truth," relented David, feeling like he had just been snookered into delivering a line from a 'B' movie.

"Very good. I'll be in touch."

Chapter 11

It's A Disease

"This is far too simplistic," objected Andy Butler.

"I'm finding it helpful," said David. Ed sat back in a corner of the room, watching Alice run through her presentation. It was 8:15 a.m. and they were sitting in the conference room next to David's office that had been set up for Ed and his team of three data crunchers. In addition to Alice, David had found two other analysts, Mark Keen, a middle aged man from manufacturing, and Chris Harned, a recently minted MBA from distribution who was two years into the corporate rotational program. They sat at the end of the table poised over their laptops.

"Just making a list of customers by revenue and giving them grades like this, A, B, and C?" asked Andy.

"Sales never went through the exercise," said David.

"May I say something?" said Alice.

"Fire away," said David.

"The point of this paper—"

"Which I never authorized," blustered Andy.

"The point of this paper was to show how little information we have about our customers."

"If anything, we have too much information. It's pouring out of the ERP, now that we have it working properly," bellowed Andy.

"But is it always useful information, or just a lot of data?" asked Ed. "Is it information that your management team and employees can put to use on a daily

IMPROVEMENT OPPORTUNITIES   Review Alice's Complete Presentation On-Line at www.smashing-silos.com

basis? Has the company analyzed the data to gain new insights, or simply used it to create the same reports that you had with the old systems? That's where the opportunities lie—in using the data to achieve a new level of insight."

"Let me just say, Andy," interjected David, "that I think that you and your team have done a tremendous job improving the efficiency of our reporting, and the quality of our company financial statements. I had a chance to look back at how it worked even two years ago, and the quality and timeliness of the data coming together seems to have improved significantly. What I think Alice has done, which has been useful to me, is assemble our data in a new way. But it's a credit to the new system that she can do this." Andy sat back and folded his arms, defensive still but somewhat appeased. "It's helping me think about where we need to get to."

Ed stood up and walked over to where Alice was standing.

"Do you mind?" he said, and took the control of the slide deck. He whipped through a few panels before stopping on the chart she had included in her report.

"This is where we start: the Pareto chart—the cumulative distribution of sales by customer, starting on the left with the largest customer and adding

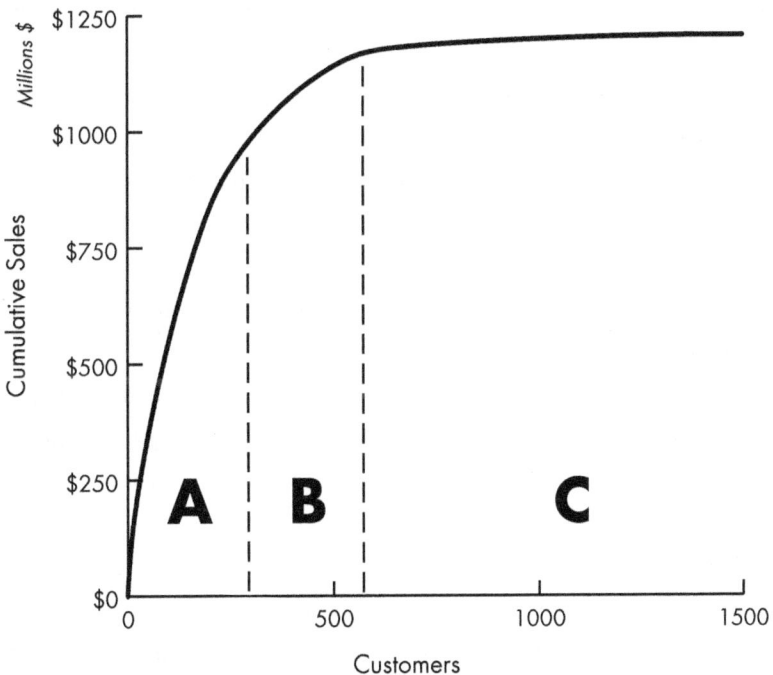

customers one by one until we get to the smallest. These A customers here make up eighty percent of your revenue. The B customers contribute another sixteen percent, and all the rest, all these C customers, generate just four percent of your top line. The obvious question we need to ask is 'Do we actually make any money serving all these smaller accounts?' To answer that question, we're going to need to allocate your expenses down to your customers at a much more granular level, right down to the line item of an every invoice."

"But we generate thousands of invoices a month," objected Andy once again.

"Don't worry, Andy, I don't expect you to do it by hand. I may have some gray hair, but I'm not that old school," joked Ed, eliciting a few chuckles from the data jockeys in the back of the room.

"Of course, of course, but it's just that we have a well-established methodology for allocating direct and indirect costs. We adhere to every policy handed down to us from corporate and we've received the highest performance review rating each of the past three years. It's very standard, and it's working for us."

"I understand your approach is probably standard, but whether or not it's working is part of what we're trying to sort out," challenged Ed. "Why don't you start by walking us through the current approach?"

"Again, it's pretty straight forward," said Andy. "Let's start with direct costs, because that's where the new ERP has made such an improvement. We're able to assign transactional costs like our product costs, standard delivery rates, and sales commissions to each sale. It lets our sales people know what kind of contribution margin they're generating."

"OK," said Ed, this time with a little more encouraging tone in his voice. "How about the indirect expenses?"

"We generate P&Ls at the sales region level. The sales personnel and the related budgets are managed by the general manager of each region, so they're direct to him or her. We allocate other operating expenses, such as marketing, research and development, human resources, and IT, according to the region's pro-rata share of the sales volume. If a region does twenty-five percent of the sales, it gets allocated twenty-five percent of the expenses."

"What about corporate overhead, like legal, accounting, and all the money they're paying David over here," asked Ed.

"There's really nothing that the regional GM can do about those expenses, so we don't burden their P&Ls with it," replied Andy. "Our attitude has always been to have them focus on what they control."

"I know where you're coming from, Andy, and you're certainly right that your approach is both very common, and fully compliant with all the accounting rules. However, your current approach is limited in two ways, both of which are critically important to driving business performance. Let's talk through it."

"OK," replied a somewhat battered Andy Butler. "Help me understand the alternative."

"First, unallocated costs," started Ed. "With COGS, delivery, and commission allocated to each transaction, you're loading less than half of the cost of the business into the contribution margin for the sale. Even after allocating most of the other operating expenses to the general managers at the regional level, you're still leaving twenty-plus percent unassigned. It's no wonder why everyone around here thinks everything is going great. If you think that contribution margin or sales region profitability is the bottom line, it is going great. Unfortunately, it's fully-loaded profitability that matters, and the only way to improve it is to show everyone the numbers, and get everyone focused on them."

The strength of Ed's convictions had the room's full attention as he continued. "Second issue: granularity. Producing financial statements at the regional level provides some insights for the GM, but it's generally not actionable for the sales people, product managers, and other managers. We need to get down to the customer level, for instance, to understand how our costs stack up against the revenue on Alice's Pareto chart."

"We've done plenty of cost-accounting exercises, Ed. It always comes down to the same thing. Is there any benefit to trying to be more precise? We could go down level after level to get to pennies. But it has never made any sense."

"Now it will, Andy, because we're going to teach the sales people and many others in the company exactly how to use this information to drive profitability. We're going to show them the levers that they can control, and make them accountable for optimizing them," said Ed.

"But we've got to begin with this picture that Alice has drawn for us," he continued. "And we need to get into the weeds to understand its implications. We need to figure out who is costing what."

"But transaction by transaction?" said Andy. "Come on. That's just making work. If it's customer profitability we're after, why not just focus at that level."

Ed grabbed a marker and stepped to the whiteboard, determined to get Andy on board with his profitability modeling approach. "When you allocate costs down to the invoice line item level, you're really allocating them to customers' accounts, customers' locations, product lines, individual SKUs, distribution centers, regions, sales people, and more...all at once. All the information on the invoice is effectively another dimension that you can use to reassemble your financials any way you'd like. You can pivot the results along a variety of axis, and, importantly, it will always tie to your company's income statement."

"We want the employees of Surgitec to know that what they do each day is directly linked to the numbers that appear in the financial statements," described David. "Right now, I'd be amazed if they could draw a line between what they do and how it affects profitability. And it's not their fault; they've been focused on other operating metrics because that's currently all they can see and control. All these other expenses seem meaningless on the front line."

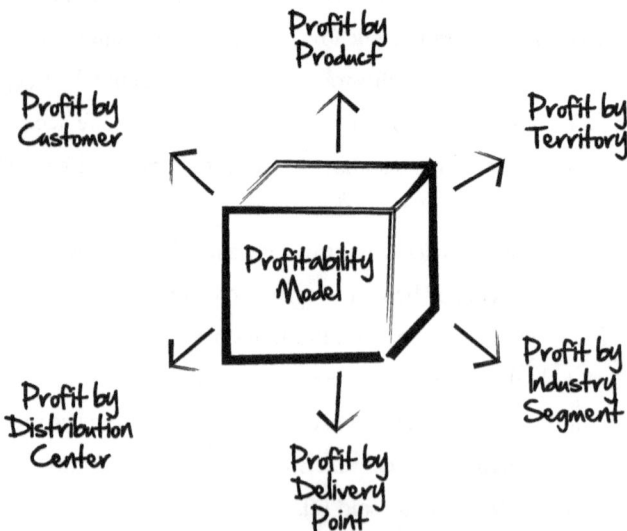

"I still don't know about this, David," complained Andy. "My organization has a pretty full plate with our existing projects and now we're supposed to report on individual customers and even invoices? Our obligation is to report company-wide performance, because that's what senior managers are here to deliver—company-wide performance."

Before David could come to Andy's rescue, Ed continued his pitch. "So let's walk through a hypothetical transaction to illustrate how powerful this concept is. Let's say a hospital buys ten thousand dollars' worth of medical supplies. You charge the cost of goods, plus delivery and commissions, directly against the sale." Andy nodded. "Then for all the indirect expenses—the marketing, R&D, sales costs, HR, IT, etcetera—what do you do?"

"Like I said, we don't do anything for that transaction. It's included in the sales volume for the region. We look at that at the end of each quarter and assign costs proportionally."

"So, again, hypothetically, if total revenue is one million dollars, you'll allocate one percent of indirect costs to this ten thousand dollar sale. Right?"

"Sure," replied Andy, "but again we don't operate at that level for every transaction."

"There will be some instances where it makes sense for you to directly charge expenses to specific transactions, like a custom configuration of a product, for instance, but I'm certainly not advocating that for every sale. My point is for *that* ten thousand dollar sale of supplies, there are likely many factors that make that one percent allocation either too much or too little. We need to consider how many locations they were shipped to, what channel was used to make the sale, how much support is required for that product category, and how much marketing spend is applied to that territory. Further, we need to make sure that the deal covers its fair share of the corporate overhead that's currently unallocated. We need this extra precision to know if this order is actually making money for Surgitec. Once you achieve this level of transparency, your sales people will be able to truly manage to the bottom line."

"Listen, I took a beating for suggesting our salespeople stay in Days Inns rather than Ritz Carltons. Now you want me to go after them about cutting costs on specific sales?"

"Is this just about cutting cost, David?" asked Ed. David looked up from his notes.

"No, Ed. No. This is about profitability. But I can understand Andy's reservations. There's a lot any business could do with perfect data. But it's not a luxury we always have. But, Andy, I think Ed's making a good point. Isn't there a way, just this once, to build up the data the way he's proposing?"

"It's a lot of work," said Andy.

"But we've assembled these great people here in the room to knock it out, right?" said David.

"I guess." All the eyes in the room were now on Andy. "Let me see what I can do."

"Great, Andy. Thanks for playing ball on this," said Ed. "Let me take you through the process that we're going to use to build the model so that you understand what data we'll need to access." Ed started back toward the whiteboard, slowly transforming from salesman to instructor as Andy began to cooperate. He added the inputs to the profitability model in his diagram.

"For starters, we need a data file with all the sales transactions for the last twelve months," said Ed. "For every transaction, it will give us the customers, the ship-to location, the distribution center, the sales rep, the products, the list price, the discounts, the quantity, and so on. Once we have those properly organized, we can work our way back up to tie them to your official financial statements. This is no challenge to the accuracy of the financial statements. We're going to get to the same numbers, and with any luck, find some opportunities to recover margin."

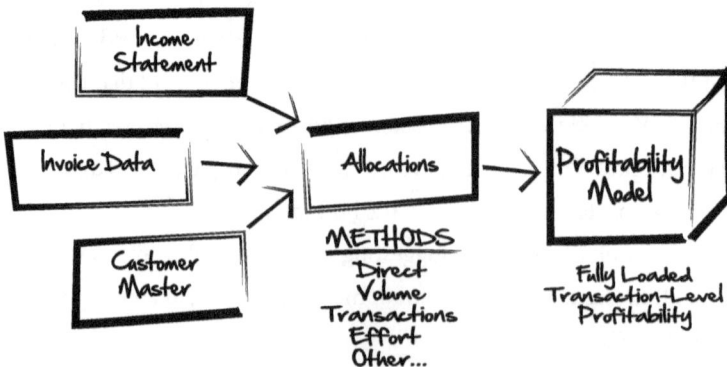

"That's a pretty simple query from the ERP," Andy admitted, "but it's going to be hundreds of thousands of rows of data...maybe even millions."

"No problem," said Chris, full of geeky bravado.

"From there, we'll want to tie the customers back to the customer master file so we can include parent account relationships, industry segments, sales person assignments, and more," said Ed.

"You'll have fun with that one, too, guys," snickered Andy. "Even after we tried to cleanse the data for the ERP implementation, the customer master is still a mess."

"The customer master has been a challenge in every business I've been in," commented David. "It's the nature of the information, and the fact that sales typically owns it, that makes it so difficult to maintain. Nonetheless, we'll have to make the most of it."

"Next, we need to get as much transaction specific cost from the ERP as we can," continued Ed. "We need COGS, freight, commissions—everything we can apply to a customer—to make the model as granular as possible. We'll then need to associate those costs to invoices in our model. Of course, in an organization this size, we can't allocate every last cent. But we can certainly do better."

"The real work is going to begin when we start allocating all the operating expenses to the transactions," offered David. "It seems we've only allocated down to the regional level to date, so we'll need to think carefully about those allocation rules."

"David's right," added Ed. "We need to think about transaction counts, unit volume, and the effort we expend as individuals and as a company to deliver the revenue. We've got to be flexible. Many companies allocate expense to customers just as you do, to regions based on volume; if a customer buys six percent of the volume, that customer gets six percent of the expenses. This approach penalizes large customers that may be very efficient to serve, and rewards smaller customers that require just as much effort. We need to develop some quick 'activity-based' rules to better allocate these expenses. Simply blending in the number of transactions is a good starting point, and then we can get more sophisticated as we progress."

"At other companies, I've used surveys to try to understand the levels of employee effort required for different transactions," said Alice, offering her first comments since Ed and Andy began their debate. "It takes a while, but you can be more precise. For example, if the billing group has to spend eighty percent of its time on direct customers, and only twenty percent on distributors, then the direct customers should be charged with that much more of the billing group's costs. Once you have this kind of data, you can really see which customers are costing you the most."

"That's a great example, Alice," said David. "I know we can't do everything. I know there are limits. But what I'd like to see is some effort in this direction. We've got a few weeks. Let's see how far we can go in allocating expenses down to the invoice level. Let's see if we can create cost buckets and then find a way to apply every single cost, so every bucket is empty by the end and we're fully reconciled with the corporate financials. Let's reconnect here in two weeks for a look at what you've built."

"We've worked on determining contribution margins for certain products in the past, and allocated distribution, sales, R&D, and marketing expenses to the product sales," noted Andy. "But beyond that, I struggle to see the value. The rest of the expenses are going to be there regardless."

"Any time you fail to allocate an expense to a transaction, you risk not fully recovering that expense, and thus risk not making a profit on that sale," said Ed. "If you become convinced that you can't charge the customer any more, than you have to question whether you can afford your overhead. Nonetheless, if you don't fully load the transaction, you, and your sales force, are flying blind."

"Flying blind doesn't sound very attractive, now does it," quipped David, drawing some tentative snickers from around the table.

As the group started to disperse, Ed offered Andy some additional assurances. "You know that the income statement we generate through our modeling effort will tie to the corporate financial statements published from your group. It's critically important that the model reconcile to your income statements so that the team knows it's a valid decomposition of the results."

"That's good to know, and it sounds like you'll be helping us get a better return out of our ERP investment," said Andy "It will be good to put all that data to use, although I'll warn you, it's a bit of a maze."

"If it's a maze," said Alice, "we'll just have to start laying some string through it."

Alice sat on the edge of the chair facing David's desk, a cup of coffee in one hand, a manila file in the other. She smoothed out the front of her skirt with the edge of the file. Ed sat in the seat beside her.

"That was a great piece of work you did, segmenting out customers by revenue. What prompted you to do it?"

"It's my job, isn't it? Planning and financial analysis."

"Of course. But no one else had looked at the issue the same way."

"I guess I had a hunch," said Alice.

"How come?"

"In my last job, I did a lot of cost accounting."

"We do a lot of cost accounting at Surgitec."

"Yes, and we did it in some really ugly situations. With companies that were in real trouble. I'm not saying Surgitec's in the same position. Nothing close. But you don't want to find out too late."

"What do you mean?"

"I guess no one plans on going out of business. It kind of creeps up on you. Sometimes, there's nothing you can do about it. Markets change, the economic climate changes. But other times, if you'd really known what was going on soon enough, you might have been able to change course."

"You did bankruptcies?"

"Unfortunately."

"Why unfortunately?"

"I'm not a confrontational person, Mr. Hewitt. And bankruptcies are usually pretty sad situations. People are trying to claw every last nickel out of what's left. It's doesn't leave you with a lot of faith in humanity."

"I see you went to Penn State. You from Pennsylvania?"

"Wilkes-Barre."

"You ever go back?"

"My family's still there. My dad owns a few muffler stores. He's done pretty well. But he's like me. He counts the pennies."

"Well, look. I wanted to say I was impressed. I know Surgitec is a fine business full of great people, but I want it to be a great business full of good people. I think the process Ed is laying out for us is going to help us get there."

"The power of numbers, I guess," said Alice. "If we can get the numbers right, everything else will follow. Everyone judges a business by its financial statements, so it's our job to understand how those numbers are optimized."

"Couldn't have put it better myself. Thank you Alice Miles of Wilkes-Barre," said Ed with a smile.

"Thanks for the opportunity."

"You created it for yourself," said David. Chris Harned and Mark Keen entered the room and David waved them toward two seats. "So what did you find out about those IVs in Texas?

Chris passed a sheet of paper to Alice, who scanned it and then slid it across David's desk.

"We sold seventeen of them for fifteen hundred dollars each," Chris said.

"Larry told me we sold sixty or eighty," questioned David.

"We're still holding eighty-three in inventory."

"And how much did they cost to make?"

"COGS was thirteen hundred and twenty-seven dollars. But manufacturing reported they had to reset their machinery to make the devices and then reset it again to go back to what they were making before. There was no way they hit their standard costs of the subsequent units after having to re-tool like that."

"How long did the re-tooling take?"

"Three hours each time."

"What had to be halted on the production line?"

"All of our standard IV equipment."

"Larry told me that he had researchers working on this for several weeks. Let me see." David flicked through his notes. "Yes, here we go. Four or five technicians over a couple of weeks. Fifty thousand to a hundred thousand dollars tops. So now you're telling me that in addition to the R&D cost, there was a large extra manufacturing cost, an inventory holding cost, and we ended up selling far fewer than we thought?"

"Yes," said Alice.

"And how important is this hospital as a customer?"

"It's a 'C' customer."

"And we spent, what, close to a quarter of a million dollars to please a 'C' customer?"

"So, here's the question, David," said Ed, rising from his chair. "Is this is an isolated symptom? Or does it suggest a broader disease?"

"Can you do the same analysis on more products, Alice?" asked David.

"Sure."

"Let's say the last twelve months. New products that required manufacturing changes, price, COGS, volume, customer." Alice tapped the criteria into her laptop.

"But don't limit it to that," said Ed. "Our bigger purpose here is to allocate costs to revenues so we get a fully loaded P&L for every customer and product. If you find something else along the way that seems relevant, build it in."

"I think you're over-estimating the change-over cost on our production lines," said Mark Keen, the analyst assigned from manufacturing. "It doesn't cost nearly so much as Alice thinks."

"So how much is it?" said David.

"It's required flexibility. You'd have to pay for it anyway."

"What do you mean?"

"We build in a certain amount of change-over costs every month to account for this kind of thing. We know that sales or R&D are going to want to make adjustments as the month goes on, so it's already budgeted for."

"On whose budget?"

"Manufacturing."

"So you're loaded with the cost of sales and R&D making these on-the-fly changes?"

"You could look at it like that. But I've spent twenty years at Surgitec, and I can tell you that last minute changes and product adjustments are just part of how a company like this functions. We need to be flexible to serve our customers."

"But does any of the support we provide to a customer get applied to that customer when we're trying to figure whether they're profitable or not?"

"Not as such."

"You mean, it gets charged against revenue along with all the other manufacturing cost."

"That's how accounting does it."

"Is it the same in distribution, Chris?"

"We allocate cost based on volume, sure," said Chris Harned, the analyst from distribution.

"But what if one customer has higher delivery costs than another?"

"Sales sets a price including delivery and we execute. Whatever the cost ends up being gets charged against revenue on the P&L."

"OK, Chris," said David, staring at the ceiling. "I get that. But internally, how do you figure out how much each one costs to serve."

"Accounting doesn't ask us to do that. Like I said, sales tells us what they've agreed to regarding delivery and service, and we execute as efficiently as we can."

"Can you find this out for me? How much did it cost to deliver those new IV systems to Texas?"

"Sure. I can probably get that for you."

"Good, then I'll be back this afternoon and we can go over this then."

The giant brick of onion rings loomed up at Ed and David from the table.

"You have an Applebee's in Paris?"

"No Applebee's. Though the French do love McDonalds. It's one of their dirty secrets."

"It amazes me that they'd consider this a portion for one person." They began picking at the intimidating heap with their forks. "How are you feeling so far?"

"I thought this morning went well. But I guess this is just the beginning."

"You're right. Getting the data straight is just part of the process. You're going to have a lot of work to do with your executives."

"I can only imagine."

"If you can get all of them to come along with this, it'll be a miracle."

"Thanks for the encouragement."

"Once we have the profitability model built, you're going to have to use the data to persuade each of your operational managers to develop hypotheses for improving the business," said Ed.

"Why's that going to be such a problem?"

"Because every time you tell someone to improve, it implies that they've been no good up to now."

"That's not true," objected David.

"OK. Not always. But when you're the new guy coming in, I can bet you there'll be people thinking exactly that. They'll be thinking they've seen it all before. They'll attack how you put together the data, how you reach conclusions, everything. Even if they don't attack you overtly, they'll be thinking it."

"What do you suggest I do," asked David.

"Accept it. Accept that you're trying to be honest and clear-eyed about this business and if that's too much for some people, it'll be more than enough for others. You don't have to be aggressive about this, David, just consistent and fair. You're not making decisions based on hunches or gut, or bias. You're trying to get to the right outcome with the data you already have. So you take what you have, and make the best possible business case you can. You'll bring along everyone you need."

"Simple as that," asked David, a bit sarcastically.

"I didn't say simple, but what I am saying is that if you get the profitability model right, you're going to be able to make discreet, surgical changes that will yield big results. The business case you assemble will get you the buy in to make the changes. Sure there's going to be some emotion along the way. There always is. But if the work you've done up to that point hasn't given you confidence, either you've done it wrong, or you're in the wrong job. Sounds easy, doesn't it?"

"Sounds like a root canal. But tell me, what are you looking for?"

"Babyback ribs?" interrupted the waitress.

"Right here," said Ed. "The salad, I'm afraid, is for him."

"If you'd been eating French food for two years, you'd want a salad."

Once they had begun eating, Ed leaned across and began talking rapidly and intensely. "But what I'm really after is facts, quantitative data. You'd think that with all the technology companies now have at their disposal, they'd all be running their businesses on data. But what you find is that these companies are run by fiefdoms, where you acquire power by waving your arms around and articulating a qualitative story. George was a master at it. He was a quite a pitchman."

"I picked that up from his letter."

"These kinds of executives loathe detail. The quicker they can get back to hand-waving the better. It's why people love them. But my approach, at the outset, is to break everything down to a highly discrete level. And once we've got all the pieces spread out on the floor, to reassemble the puzzle so it makes sense. Here's the paradox. Executives say they want a simple management structure, so historically they compartmentalize operations by function. But when then those simple compartments aren't coordinated or disciplined, they actually create more complexity. Instead, top executives should really be pushing more data and metrics across departments, and help their managers use them to coordinate and monitor their activities. That's how they could make their jobs simpler, as they could get the whole organization focused on fewer, higher-level objectives. But really, what do you think executives want more than anything else, David?"

"To succeed, I guess. To run a profitable, sustainable business."

"Just that?'

"To make a good living for themselves."

"Sure. But you know what I find executives want more than anything? To be liked and admired. It's a natural tendency. Who wants to be disliked? They don't want to inconvenience anyone. But then when you need to do something hard, you have to inconvenience people. It's an intellectual and emotional conflict. But if you never bother to resolve it, you'll never escape the quagmire."

"You're full of theories, Ed."

"They used to be theories. But they're not anymore. I've seen it too many times. And I'm going to see it again here. Trust me."

There was a single sheet of paper waiting for David on his desk when he returned from lunch. It was a memo from Chris.

"Seventeen IV systems were delivered to Texas in March. They were sent overnight express on a truck from South Carolina. Total cost—nineteen hundred seventy-five dollars. Billed directly to customer—zero dollars."

It's starting to look like a disease, thought David.

Chapter 12

George Wouldn't Have Done This

"You consultants never understand sales. You think everything comes down to efficiency. You have no idea what it takes to sell—the time, the relationships built up over years." Barry brought his hand down hard on the table in his office. "You think you can measure everything and somehow everything will be neat and tidy. It's never that way. Sometimes you have to accept the world like it is."

"All I'm trying to do is understand how you get from the list price to the ultimate invoice price on a few products," said Ed while Alice took notes beside him. The team was just a couple days into their assessment and already meeting resistance.

"And what will that tell you? That we have to haggle and bargain a little to make sales? That it takes flexibility to maintain our unit volume?"

"Just the various steps. That's all," said Ed, maintaining his composure.

"I'm going to have to talk to David about this. This is minutia. It would never have happened under George."

"Sure, but why don't we just start with these surgical dressings. Five cases sold to the Lincoln Community Hospital in Nebraska. List price $445 a case. Invoice price, $254. Why the steep discount?"

"We're going to sit here and argue over twelve hundred bucks, give or take?"

"We don't need to argue, but we do need to understand how the prices and discounts work," responded Alice.

"OK. Let me take a look. So, this is one of our biggest customers in the Midwest, and a very strategic customer given that they do work with the University. Their standard discount is thirty-six percent."

Ed punched away at his calculator. "Hmm, we've still got thirty-one bucks to go."

"They always pay within thirty days, so for that we take off 2 percent."

"Just for paying on time?" said Ed.

"As I said, we've been doing it this way with them for years. They're a huge customer."

"Still got another twenty-two dollars per case by my math," said Ed.

"Let's see what product they bought," said Barry, focusing on the details of the invoice. "This is a new product for us. Just introduced it last year. Market offered an incentive to get people using it."

"How much?" asked Ed.

"Another five percent"

"So that brings us to forty-three percent," calculated Alice.

"They're incentives. You know how many choices they have out there? They could drop us any minute and it would be a huge hit to our top line." Barry's voice began to rise as he spoke.

"How much?" asked Ed.

"Two…two and a half million dollars."

"What's the operating margin we make on Lincoln Community Hospital?"

"Same as we make across the company. But as I said, they pay a lot of bills."

"So, you don't have an estimate of net margins by customer."

"No. I could tell you by sales zone."

"That's a start."

Barry pulled out a file from behind his desk and flipped through. "Here you go. Plains zone, gross margin Q1, fifty percent."

"That's in line with the rest of company, but what about the operating margins? What's it look like after all our operating expenses?"

"I don't know," said Barry. "Maybe a couple points offs given the size of the territory. But still, I'm sure it's positive. It's a huge market for us, the Midwest. What are we going to do, stop selling there?"

"Well," Ed said to Alice a few minutes later, as they left the meeting. "If we're handing out forty-three percent in discounts just to keep the business flowing, we might need to think about it."

"I understand, Barry, I really do," said David. Barry was steaming in the chair on the other side of his desk. David could tell he needed to vent.

"We've had these consultants here before; they come in, thinking they know our business."

"I understand. But I'm telling you this is different and I want you on board."

"On board the Titanic. We've got this Ed guy and his teenage sidekick from finance asking me to justify the price of a bunch of bandages. You think I don't know whom we charge what and why? It's all up here, David," he said tapping his skull. "It's been up here for twenty-seven years, and it's stayed up here through all those botched ERP implementations and all those millions we've flushed away. They keep trying to turn sales into some kind of technology and accounting control project, but it is what it is; it's about people and relationships and how you manage them. No bunch of consultants with their little questionnaires and spreadsheets are going to change that."

"Barry, this process is going to go ahead. No one around here doubts that you are an excellent salesman and sales manager. You have a great team, great customers, and a great track record. But we have to face some realities. Surgitec's returns are not what Carson expects. As a business unit, Surgitec has been underperforming, and what's frightening is that no one around here seems to be able to tell me why."

"We'll do better when these new customers we're winning start to grow."

"Volume is not the problem, Barry. It's our margins. Building ever more volume around the same model does not solve the problem."

"So what, you want us to fire customers?"

"Perhaps, but first I'd like to know which of our customers are profitable and which aren't. That's why I've asked Ed to help us dig into our pricing practices. I want to know, customer by customer, whether we're charging what we should and what we could."

"Sure, you can know all that, but we've been doing things a certain way and if you're going to start tearing apart every single customer relationship we have, then it's going to cause a lot of trouble with my sales team, and with our customers…"

"We're not in this to keep everyone trouble-free and happy, Barry. We run Surgitec to make a return in line with Carson's goals. If we can't, it'll be up to another company and another group of people to do what you suggest and not make trouble."

"I understand that, David," said Barry. "I might be a good ole' boy salesman, but I read the news too. I know this is blood sport, and that the numbers matter. I'm just trying to make sure we don't lose all our customer relationships in the process."

"Barry, what I need you and your team to do with those customer relationships is make them profitable. It may take some adjustments to discount rates, or some changes to their delivery terms, and it might be a tough conversation to have. But we need to get your team on board with the fact that every customer relationship must be *profitable*," said David.

"I suppose that's pretty tough to argue with. None of my guys want their customers to lose money for Surgitec," said Barry.

"I'm sure they don't. So we're going to make sure they have the information and the authority they need to fix the problems."

"We can get this done, David," said Barry, as his natural competitiveness and appetite for challenge started to kick in.

"Great, I thought you'd come around." David got up and strolled to the whiteboard. "And I'll tell Ed that we've agreed on our second strategic imperative."

Strategic Imperative #2:
Remedy Unprofitable Customer Relationships

The two men stood up and shook hands. "By the way," asked Barry, "what's everyone else saying about this process?"

"You know this company better than I do," said David.

"How's Laura taking cost allocation?"

"You can guess."

"You can't put a price on the brand," mocked Barry.

"Exactly." Barry laughed for the first time in the meeting. "I want you to run Surgitec's sales, Barry, but I need you to look at how you run it and make sure we're doing it in a way that gets our returns to where they need to be. I want you here, but I want to make sure you're with me. In any case, if we can't improve our returns, this whole discussion will have been a waste of time, because we'll all be looking for work elsewhere."

"It's not going to be pretty," warned Barry.

"I know. I don't need it to be."

"Over here, Mr. Hewitt," shouted Chuck Long, the head of distribution. He had to raise his voice to be heard above the noise of four Surgitec trucks starting their engines. They were parked, loaded, and ready to leave from the company's warehouse five miles from the Harleysville headquarters. They were obviously maintained with great care, painted cream with Surgitec written across the side in navy blue. The hubcaps gleamed. The metal fittings on the cab shone in the morning sunshine. The four truck drivers wore jeans and blue Surgitec shirts and were signing various forms before they began their day's work.

David walked over to where Chuck was standing. Chuck handed him a hard hat and a safety vest similar to the ones being worn by the drivers.

"So, where are these going?" David said, leaning into Chuck's ear.

"All over the north and northeast—to hospitals, clinics, and some of our larger private practice groups." They stepped aside to avoid a forklift truck delivering a pallet load of surgical gloves to one of the trucks. Chuck looked down at his clipboard. "Boston, Chicago, Rochester, and the fourth one's going up to Montreal."

"How many trucks are going out today?"

"We've got twenty going out of here, around the same operating out of our warehouse in South Carolina."

"Do they bring anything back on their return trips?"

"No, only returns if there are any."

"What about the West?"

"We ship from South Carolina by train, mostly, to hubs in Fort Worth and Chicago, and go from there to serve the Western states."

"And Latin America?"

"Ships out of Puerto Rico. For high end product we don't manufacture down there, we might fly it out of South Carolina. Come on, hop in." Chuck led him over to the cab of one of the trucks. "David, meet Eddy. Hey Eddy, how long have you been with Surgitec?"

"Twenty-seven years, Chuck." Eddy was a small man with a jockey's build, lean face, and with a slight stoop from so many years behind the wheel. David shook his hand, which felt like a discarded leather glove, rough and limp.

"Mr. Hewitt here is the new CEO."

"Course he is, Chuck. You think just because we drive the trucks we don't know these things. Nice to meet you, Sir."

"He wanted to see how we operate." Eddy turned and opened his hands, wide.

"Here you have it, Sir. The trucks come in, the trucks go out." The other drivers standing around laughed.

"How about you show me your cab?" said David, side-stepping any awkwardness.

"Happy to, Sir." Eddy jumped gingerly from the loading dock and walked over to the door. David followed. Eddy scrambled up the step on the passenger's side then slid across the bench. David climbed in and left the door open so the driver's gathering below could hear their conversation. The first thing that struck him was how tidy it was. He recalled driving trucks as a college student and they were uniformly filthy, reeking of tobacco and unwashed days on the road.

There were a few photographs tacked to the dashboard. "Grandkids?" said David looking at a picture of a baby splashing in a pool.

"Kids. Didn't get married till I was forty-five."

"What were you waiting for all those years?"

"I was on the road for Surgitec. Never had much time. My wife was a nurse at one of the downtown hospitals in Philadelphia. Ran into her a few times on my route. That's how it happened. Same with a lot of the guys who work here. Now I'm forty-eight years old with two children under ten. They'll be graduating high school when I'm in my late fifties."

"They'll keep you young. Your wife doesn't mind you being on the road so much?"

"She's got lots of family close by." David thought about Maria and the boys. His own mother was in Michigan, and her family was in North Carolina. Seemed like the higher you moved in a company, the more isolated you became. Even the truck drivers at Surgitec had more balance between their work and family life than he did. He looked behind the seats and saw a neatly made bed, narrow but clean, and more than enough for a man of Eddy's size. Above it was a small television set. Below that was a narrow shelf arranged with Surgitec files and brochures.

"You still use those?"

"Sometimes. We're mostly computerized these days." From a compartment in front of the passenger's seat, he pulled out a tablet device. "We enter the information in here. The terminal monitors our routes, to make sure we're not sneaking off. They keep track of where we are, how much fuel we're using. Then the loads themselves have tracking devices, so we can be sure we've delivered everything at the right place."

"So why the files?"

"For some of the smaller customers. They still like to do things on paper. Invoices, acknowledgements of receipt. Then I normally give them a few brochures."

"Isn't that sales' job?"

"We all do our bit. Sometimes the sales guys come and go, but I've been delivering to some of the same customers since I joined. They know me better than they do the guys who sell to them. I'm not explaining products, just giving them information."

"Does Chuck ask you to do this?"

"No. It's just me. My uncle used to drive for the company. He did the same thing."

David and Chuck walked through the immaculately kept warehouse, past towering boxes of product. David could see the conveyor belts bringing them in and dropping them into loading areas. Fork-lifts spun at high speed around the space, but beside the drivers, there were surprisingly few people. Some were doing spot checks of orders, but most of the work had been mechanized.

Chuck's office was on the floor of the warehouse. It's white walls were decorated with dozens of old photographs showing the evolution of Surgitec's distribution system, from early motorized trucks to today's modern fleet. The photographs showed generations of Surgitec drivers and warehouse workers wearing their blue uniforms with the white Surgitec logo. One photograph showed a picture of a huge port, lit up at night, with two ships loaded up with Surgitec containers.

"Where's this?" asked David.

"Panama," said Chuck. "We ship our containers from there. We service our Central and Latin American markets by sea."

"Interesting, we go by sea to Central and Latin America?"

"Done it that way for thirty years. Best way of guaranteeing our product gets to market. It's more sophisticated now, but thirty years ago, it was really the only way to get product down there with any sense of reliability. Take a seat."

"Is it very expensive shipping that way?"

"By sea? Not really, it is actually less expensive than air."

"What about trucking or rail?"

"It's competitive with both trucking and rail and it is much more reliable, especially since many of the big markets, and our distribution centers, are located along the coast."

"Glad to hear it."

"Years ago, the alternatives weren't as evolved. Air shipping was still too expensive, and the roads through South America were a mess. Anyway, how's it all going with the big review I keep hearing about?"

"We're making progress. It's never easy coming in somewhere new and trying to figure out all that's going on."

"Tell me about it."

"But we're digging in. So I'd like to hear it from you."

"From the horse's mouth."

"Exactly."

Chuck sat down heavily on his creaking leather chair and rocked backwards hard. David thought for a moment it might collapse beneath him. Chuck drank from a large can of sweetened iced tea.

"Like I told you when we first met, our key metric is customer satisfaction."

"Since when?"

"Since forever. It's been like this as long as I've been at Surgitec. Those guys you see on the walls, the drivers and deliverymen, they're the soul of this company. They get out there and meet the customers. They talk to the doctors and nurses, the supply room managers, the buyers. They're the face of this company. Always have been. Won't change as long as I'm here."

"Of course. How many are there?"

"As of today, let me look," he picked up a school exercise book and flicked through the pages. "One hundred seventy-three drivers, one hundred forty-seven in warehouse operations, and fifty-four in logistics and support. What's that, three hundred and seventy-four in total working directly in distribution."

"That includes overseas?"

"Yes. But only those directly employed by us. You probably double that if you include those employed by our logistics partners but who work almost full time for us."

"And how do you measure customer satisfaction?"

"We do two annual surveys, questionnaires. We measure on-time delivery and inventory stock-outs. There are far fewer stock-outs since we implemented the new inventory management module with the ERP, because it measures average usage by our customers and gives us advance warning of when they're going to run out. It's cut down a lot on express deliveries. We know ahead of time when they're going to need a delivery. Big difference. This year, we had ninety percent of our customers tell us they were 'very satisfied' with our delivery. We had a ninety-eight percent 'on-time' record and inventory stock-outs were down eighteen percent from two years ago. I can't imagine our rivals are doing as well—not even close."

"How do you determine which customers get priority?"

"Hey, every customer has a business to run, so we make sure we're there for all of them, even if we need to pull some over-time or special runs to get it done."

"And how do you cost all this?"

"You mean the quarterly budgets? We budget based on sales estimates. If we think we're going to be selling 'x' dollars, we reckon we'll need a percentage of that, based on our historical estimates, to deliver product. Then we have a separate allocation for cap-ex, updating our fleet, computer systems, and so on."

"Do you allocate cost to customers or regions?"

"Well, I can tell you where we sent our trucks."

"And match that up with the size of the delivery, fleet overtime, fuel?"

"We can probably get it."

"I think that would be a pretty useful exercise," encouraged David. "How do you charge customers?"

"We've got a freight table, based on volume, weight, region, and time. Expedited deliveries cost more, obviously."

"And what if one customer is farther away from a distribution center than another? Do they get charged more?"

"We try not to nickel and dime them like that. It's bad for the relationship."

"Do you ever find out if sales offers distribution discounts?"

"Sales often waives delivery charges, but that doesn't affect us. That's between sales and finance. Like I said, we get our budget based on volume estimates and we try to stick to it. If we deliver more than we predicted, our costs are higher, if we deliver less, they're lower."

"So what appears on the invoice is the sale price plus a delivery price based on the freight table, minus any discounts."

"You got it."

"And when you get new customers, how do you estimate the cost to serve them?"

"We do it by region. If they're here in the northeast, it's one price, if they're out West it's another, and so on."

"But the Northeast is huge, the West even more so."

"Not our business. If sales brings in a customer and improves the top line, our job is to make sure they get Surgitec products when they need them."

"What about minimum orders?"

"If sales tells us something's got to go, we take it. Like I said, it's about the customer. George had one of those sales consultants in here recently. You know, most of their jargon goes in one ear and out the other. But this guy talked about how we had to 'surprise and delight' the customer. I listened to this guy, because I realized that's what we do. We're all about surprise and delight. If one of our customers needs one surgical glove or one pack of needles, you bet we'll drive through the night to get it to them."

"Laura Chan wants a word," said Marjorie, as David returned to the office.

"She sounded pretty upset."

"OK. Let's get her on the phone." David sat down at his desk and took a deep breath as he braced for another earful about his consulting team. He picked up the receiver when it rang.

"David, I just spoke to this consultant of yours," began Laura, her voice clenched and audibly angry. "What's going on?"

"I've asked Ed to help me better understand our profitability."

"He doesn't seem to think much of marketing."

"Don't mind his manner. He's just highly focused."

"He kept asking me about cost allocation. We've never done cost allocation the way he seemed to think about it. We get our budget and we do the best job we can to meet our strategic objectives. I felt he didn't take us seriously."

No one would ever take Laura as seriously as Laura felt she deserved, thought David.

"I'm trying to get a better handle on Surgitec, Laura. Don't worry. I've been really impressed so far with what I've seen of your work."

"I've been around business a long time, David, and here's the thing about these consultants. They take your own watch and tell you the time."

"Yes, I've heard that before."

"So why are you hiring another one?"

David couldn't just say, "because Linda Thomas told me to."

"Because sometimes it's good to have a fresh perspective," he replied. "Ed is working with our team to do a level of analysis that's new for us. It's something that our internal team hasn't done before. I've been at Carson my whole career, so it's helpful to step outside for new approaches. It doesn't mean we're going to act on it, but it's useful to review."

"Glad to hear you're retaining your skepticism about this guy. He didn't seem to care about the awards we've won. He looked totally disinterested."

"It's OK, Laura. That's just the way he is."

"George would never have let a guy come in like this, telling us our house is a mess and our babies are ugly."

"I understand, Laura. Really, I do." There was a silence as Laura's anger ebbed away.

"Well, thanks for hearing me out. I appreciate it."

"Don't mention it. I'll speak to Ed."

Chapter 13

We're Not Going To Be That Company

"So I'm hearing that you guys are making friends all across the company," quipped David as the team re-assembled in the war room for their two-week update on the profitability model. Ed, Mike and Chris joined David at the conference table as Alice prepared to present.

"Yes, David, we've had a great couple weeks of really drilling down into the numbers," said Ed, oblivious to the sarcasm, or at least choosing to ignore it. "We've taken the P&L and blown it up to the nth degree. Alice, show us what you've got."

"What we've got is preliminary, but you'll be able to get a pretty clear view of what the numbers are going to tell us," began Alice. "We started with the sales data that Andy gave us, and then developed a set of rules to allocate expenses to each invoice line item. We are now able to calculate operating income for each transaction, and then roll them up to see profitability by customer. Building the income statement up from this level gives us a much different perspective on where we're profitable and where we're not."

"What's new here, David, is the specificity of the allocation rules, and the level at which we applied them," interjected Ed. "Before, expenses were just spread around at the region level based on a percentage of revenue. Now, we're going several layers deeper. We're allocating R&D and marketing proportionately to the product lines where it was spent. We're assigning distribution costs based on the specific costs of the distribution center involved, and based on the miles

CUSTOMER PROFITABILITY

Review the Team's Complete Presentation On-Line at www.smashing-silos.com

traveled to make the delivery. We're allocating some costs on a per transaction basis, and blending some rates between sales and transactions. It's a much more accurate view than we've had before, and this is only our first cut."

"So how does this differ from regular cost accounting?" asked David.

"Same idea, but again, we're getting much more granular," said Ed. "We're stripping it right back to transactions. It's like taking a house down to the studs to see where everything is. Once we roll everything up, we tie it into the corporate financial statements. There's no question here about the accuracy of those statements. We're just trying to figure out precisely how you get there."

"What we're trying to construct," said Alice, "is a matrix of customers, SKUs, revenues, and expenses so we can pivot off it and figure out what should go where. Right now, we're trying to get things directionally right."

"And when you get the data how you want it, built up by transaction, you could give me a P&L, say, for a particular product for a particular month, in a particular territory? Or a particular customer?"

"That's the plan," affirmed Alice.

"Complete visibility into the P&L," boasted Chris.

"What you've got now is the Carson system," said Ed. "A system for doing allocations and spreading dollars based on a set of rules that work well in a large corporation. What this system doesn't help you with is change. It's built to simplify accounting, but not to simplify our task of driving change."

"And it doesn't give us profitability below the highest levels." echoed David.

"Not even close. That's why everyone is focused on sales volumes and, maybe, gross margin. It's all that they can see and control," explained Ed.

"So what's it all tell us," asked David, anxious to see the hard data rather than rehash the theory.

"Here's the biggest headline," continued Alice as she clicked to her next slide. "Remember the Pareto chart of sales that we talked about a couple weeks ago. Here's what it looks like when you overlay operating income on it. It tells us that we're most profitable with just twenty-six percent of our customers, and that sixty-one percent are losing money."

"Whoa," said David as he lurched forward in his chair. "Who are they? What do we need to get them fixed?" Alice seemed to know how to get his attention!

"We had the same questions," replied Alice. "The first thing we did was look at profitability by size of customer. We segmented customers by annual purchases using the same A-B-C classification we used during our last discussion, and then looked at the P&L for each segment."

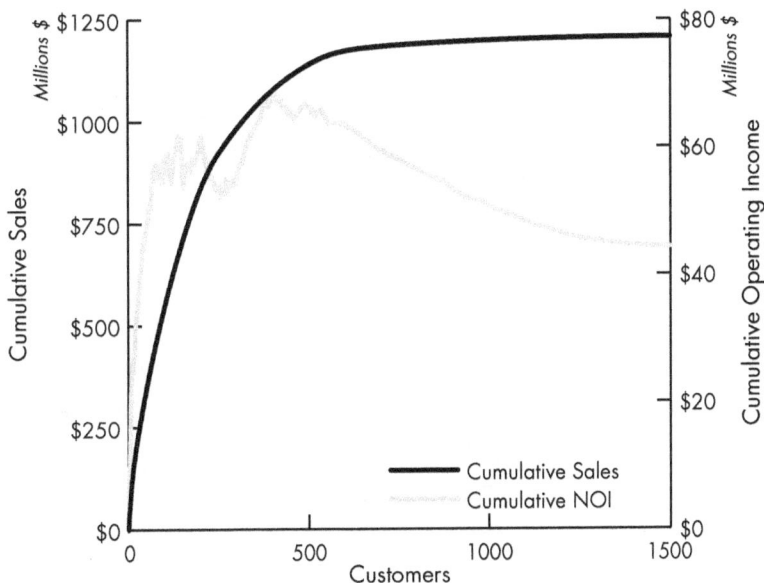

Alice clicked to the next slide and continued. "As you might expect, the 'A' customers are making the most money for us. 'A' customers average $3.4 million per year in revenue at operating margins of 5.4 percent, which is a couple points above the company average. 'B' customers aren't contributing as much profit in total, but the operating margins are a bit better."

"The problem lies with the 'C's,'" she continued. "We're absolutely getting killed with these small customers. Seventy-eight percent are unprofitable. We're losing twenty million a year on sales of forty-eight million dollars."

"It's not too surprising that we make our money on the bigger customers," said David, "but the magnitude of losses from the 'C's is staggering, and such a low percentage of profitable accounts is tough to accept."

"This is an example of where traditional sales reporting fails us," said Ed. "Most salespeople and sales managers are accustomed to thinking about

profitability in terms of gross margin, as that's typically all they've got. By
that measure, these small customers are fine, even a little better than the A
customers."

"Sales and gross margin are the metrics I've always used," confirmed David.
"That's how most of Carson runs, not just Surgitec."

"That's how most companies operate, but unfortunately it doesn't account for
all the infrastructure that you need to serve these customers. When you consider
the costs of order entry, fulfillment, delivery, invoicing, and collections, it costs
about as much to process a small order as it does a big one. Technical support
is often even more expensive, as smaller customers rely on their vendors rather
than having internal support staff," said Ed.

"When we started allocating some of the costs by the number of
transactions, rather than just a percentage of sales, we saw the losses pile up
with the small customers," said Alice. "We can get more precise with our cost
allocations over time, but we're confident that this approach is far more accurate
than what we've done in the past."

"OK, I get it," said David. "Now what do we do about it?"

"Big picture, David, we have an alignment problem," said Ed. "Surgitec has a
direct sales and distribution model designed for serving big customers, the kind
of customers that buy pallets of product, if not truck loads. On the other hand,
we have sales incentives and a corporate culture that encourages reps to bring
in as many new accounts as possible, regardless of size. All these new accounts
provide a sense that you're winning, but really you're just running up costs. Sure,
it's growth, but it's not profitable growth."

"Over ninety percent of our new business acquisition efforts last year
resulted in C customers who have little or no hope of ever being anything but C
customers," added Alice. "There's implicit motivation within our sales force to
grow the customer base, especially for junior sales people trying to notch their
first wins."

"We need to do a better job of identifying high growth, high-value segments,
and committing our resources there," she continued, "rather than scattering them
around a lot of low-growth, low-return customers. These C customers may be
better served by a distributor rather than directly by us. Our sales pipeline needs

to have profitability as its top priority."

"These are all good insights," said David, scribbling furiously on a notepad. "Barry was boasting to me about all the new customers they bring in, and Chuck was proud that they try to delight even the smallest customers. Those attitudes appear to be the problem, not the solution."

"That's likely the case," agreed Ed. "The remedy is to either dramatically de-cost the sales and distribution operation so you can make money with these small accounts, or simply stop serving them. It's counter intuitive, but sometimes the way to grow profits is to shrink sales."

"That'll be a big change for Barry, but at least we now know that our issues lie with these small accounts. We can focus our changes there," said David.

"Unfortunately, it's not that simple," cautioned Ed. "What's even more troublesome than seventy-eight percent of the 'C' customers being unprofitable is that thirty-three percent of the 'A' customers and twenty-eight percent of the 'B's are also unprofitable. There's no reason that Surgitec should be losing money on those larger accounts."

"So it's not just about the total revenue we're generating from them. There's something else that's causing them to be unprofitable," surmised David. "What's the issue?"

"There are actually two big issues: discounts and transaction costs," answered Alice. "The best way to understand what's going on is to compare the top and bottom accounts. Let's take a look at the largest customers, the 'A' customers:"

'A' Customer Metrics	Top 10	Bottom 10
Average Sales	$3.9 Million	$2.3 Million
Average Discount Rate	16%	31%
Average # of Sites	3.5	20.6
Average # of Transactions	102.5	1,526.6
Average Order Size	$38,888	$1,516
Transportation (% of Sales)	1%	43%
Net Operating Margin %	31%	(89%)

"The top ten most profitable customers generate, on average, $1.6 million more per year in sales than the bottom ten, but that's not the full story. The bigger issue is that even though we're losing money, we're still offering the bottom customers, on average, a thirty-one percent discount. Altogether, we're extending $174 million in discounts to unprofitable customers. That's almost three times our annual operating income."

"How are these discounts getting approved," asked David. "It seems that we're giving away the farm to anyone who asks."

"Again, it goes back to the reporting and the incentives," replied Ed. "The approval structure for discounts is designed to reward higher sales, so most of these big accounts qualify for steep discounts. However, they don't take into account the full cost of servicing the account; they don't consider profitability."

"And that takes us to the second part of the problem, transportation costs. On average, the bottom performing customers are ordering almost fifteen times more each year, with an average order size of just fifteen hundred bucks. The bottom customers also seem to have lots of different sites as ship-to locations, whereas the best customers are more centralized, with only a couple different ship-tos. The impact is that it's costing us significantly more to deliver to these accounts—forty-three percent of sales—and we're not able to recover it."

"Look at these big money-losing accounts, David," said Ed, as he approached the screen and waved his hand toward the bottom ten. "The annual sales revenue is pretty good on whole, but yet with small orders and multiple sites, you really need to view them as a collection of small accounts rather than one large account. They've been able to leverage their purchasing power to get an 'A' level discount, but than their behaving like a bunch of 'C' customers. It's the worst of both worlds."

"Alice, can you fast forward to that scatter diagram," directed Ed. "This chart will give you a feel for the problem, David." A new chart appeared on the screen.

"Each dot on this plot represents one of Surgitec's customers. On the bottom axis you've got their average order size for the year. Up the side you've got the discount rate we're offering them. Can you see how they're correlated?" Ed paused as David stared at the jumble of dots on the screen.

"Hmmm. I'm sorry, Ed, I'm not seeing it," replied David.

"Exactly! There is no correlation. It's totally random, but it shouldn't be.

Discounts should be a lever to get customers to behave the way you want them to behave, and a reward for profitable relationship. What you see here is that we reward just as many customers for being unprofitable, as we do for being profitable."

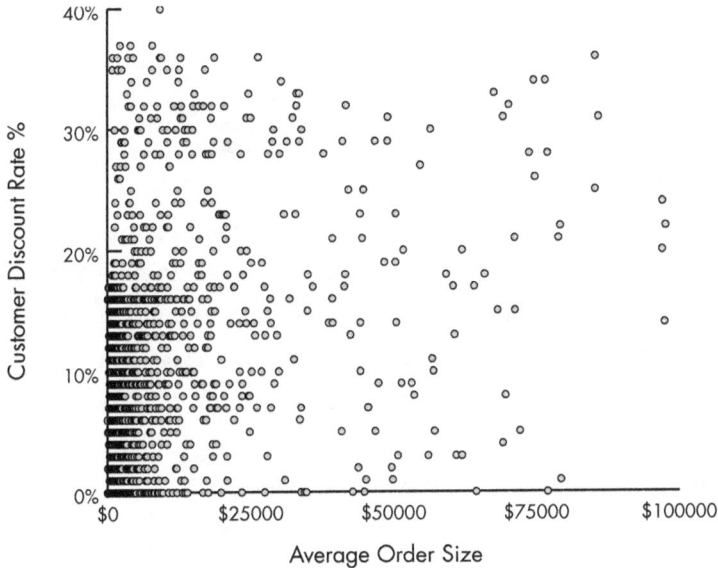

"Are you seeing the same issues across all the sales territories," asked David.

"For most part," said Chris. "The better performing regions generate more revenue per sales rep, average larger orders, and offer slightly lower discounts. They're basically microcosms of the larger trends. They also seem to be served by the most efficient distribution centers, so distribution cost is just 5.8 percent of sales in the best performing zones, versus 11.7 percent in the worst zones."

"The most profitable zones seem to be the smallest geographically," noted Alice. "Plus, the more sales a territory generates, the better they utilize the distribution center and the cheaper it becomes. It's a virtuous cycle."

"Any outliers," asked David. "Are there any territories that are big losers?"

"South America, which is mostly Argentina, is the biggest problem," replied Alice.

"What's going on there?"

"For some reason, we have a fully-staffed regional office there—twenty-five people working on marketing, sales, and distribution. Just the cost of that takes the business there from positive to negative NOI. That's all aside from currency fluctuations, the shipping costs, and the specific segment issues there. It's a huge country, so selling to one customer with multiple ship-to locations can have a big effect on the profitability of a contract."

"Tell him about the Argentine labels," prompted Ed to Mike. "That's a good example of some of our challenges in manufacturing, not just Argentina."

Mike had been silent throughout the meeting. As he began, it was clear he lacked the same enthusiasm for the process as his team mates.

"So, we sell insulin injection kits in Argentina, as we do in most of our Latin American markets. Sales won a good-sized order from a private hospital group there. But the regulations are a little different in Argentina, so R&D had to adjust the product slightly. Then we got a request from marketing to redesign the packaging so that the labels included the address of our local office in Argentina instead of the regional headquarters in Panama."

"How big was the order," asked David.

"One hundred seventy-five thousand dollars," replied Mike.

"And the costs of redesigning the products and labels?"

"Including change-over time on the production line in Puerto Rico?"

"Yes," confirmed David.

"Fully loaded, with all the costs allocated according to Ed and Alice's model, around forty-seven thousand dollars," said Mike.

"And what does that do to the profitability of the sale?"

"The model says we lost thirty thousand dollars," answered Mike. "If we accept this kind of allocation—"

"And why wouldn't we?" said David.

"We're looking at close to fifteen hundred customers here and ten thousand SKUs and sixty different columns of data. You can keep segmenting to find whatever you want and then use that to blame someone."

David ran his hand through his hair and looked up at the ceiling. "Alice, do you think Mike has a point? That we're segmenting and pivoting our way to nowhere?"

"I don't have Mike's experience. But I do think we're getting to some pretty pure data. We're not trying to obscure anything. We're trying to get a clearer view of the business."

"You ever worked in manufacturing, Alice?" asked Mike.

"No."

"You ever been on a shop floor, Chris? Seen how it works? Of course there's going to be times when machinery's under-utilized. Or moments when some guy spills his soda all over the new specs and there's an hour wasted getting a new set. But that's just part of life. You start trying allocate all of that specifically to customers and products, and Surgitec as a company will spend all its resources doing accounting instead of making things."

"But what about the data, Mike?" said Alice. "Is it wrong?"

"No, it's not wrong. It's just that when you're talking about a customer in Argentina who wants insulin kits made a certain way, you can't just look at one transaction in isolation. That customer might be growing. It might be a great customer in the future even if you lose a few dollars today. Sales might have great strategic reasons for making the investment in that customer."

"That's fine," said Alice. "But we need to know that. If that's the case, then sure we can swallow the cost now. But if it's going to be an on-going problem, then we need to know that, too. No customer can stay unprofitable forever. The data's a way for us to have this discussion."

"So what would you do about it? How would you fix this unprofitable customer?" Mike stood, his arms folded, leaning back slightly. The argument seemed to have made him even more resolute in his objection to the process.

"I'd like to ask a few questions," Alice said, jotting some notes on a sheet of paper. "First, I'd like to see if this product is worth adapting for this market. Is it worth it to make it compliant with the local regulations? I'd like to find out why we felt it was necessary to make the label change. Then I'd like to know more about this customer and market. What other products are we selling here? Do the margins on the rest of our business here justify fresh investment?"

"We already know that Argentina's a big market," said Mike.

"But we don't understand if it can be profitable for us," replied Alice.

"You know how hard it is to build a profitable regional business?" said Mike indignantly. "You understand all it involves? You seem to think that business is this clinical process, and if you just tinker with the accounts long enough, you'll find the answer."

"This is just the argument we need to be having," said David, intervening before Mike became more heated. "I appreciate what both of you are saying. Mike, you have been here a long time and understand how this business works. Ed's approach, and Alice's, is about bringing fresh eyes to familiar problems. I need you both to work together on this, because for this process to work, I need both perspectives." Mike nodded and sat down. "No company can be understood from the numbers alone. I realize that Mike. But equally, qualitative data doesn't give me all the answers either. I need both to get the visibility I want. Any company that thinks its processes are set in stone might as well just pack up and go home. We're not going to be that company. So, where do we go from here? How do we get this fixed?" David prompted his team for the next steps.

"We need to ensure that discounts, service level agreements, delivery fees, and product customizations align to the profitability of the segment, and ultimately of the customer account," answered Alice. "After working through this with Ed, we all agree that we need much more detailed account planning, both before and after signing a deal. We need the sales rep to factor in delivery frequency, number of ship-to locations, minimum order quantities and any specialized product designs that they require. And after the agreement is inked, we need to ensure that we have the right incentives, reporting, and contractual levers to manage the bottom line."

"Alice's has made some good suggestions, but remember that this is just the first version of the model," noted Ed. "Recommending a course of action is a bit premature. Chris and Mark are going to dig into the segments and the distribution centers during the next phase of the assessment. We also have to review product profitability in-depth. We'll have some more actionable analysis when we finish that work."

"OK. Sounds good," said David. "Same time next week."

"How is going?" asked David as he and Alice walked from the meeting room toward the coffee machine by the reception area.

"It's challenging."

"It's supposed to be."

"How are you finding working with Ed?"

"He's very direct."

"I thought you'd appreciate that."

"It doesn't always sit well with everyone in the company, especially when we're trying to get information out of people."

"It seems to be working, though, right?"

"I guess."

"You don't sound convinced."

"Information is where you start in a process like this, but it's not where you end. We can't go antagonizing people when we ask them for information if we're going to be back in a few weeks asking them to act on the information and change what they do."

"I see what you're saying. Is there a lot of confrontation?"

"Even if they don't say it, they're thinking it."

"Shouldn't be any problem for a woman from Wilkes-Barre."

"Is that a badge of honor," joked Alice. "You ever been there?"

"No," confessed David.

"We've got a museum dedicated to Harry Houdini."

"The escape artist?"

"Exactly. They buried him six feet under. He escaped. Strapped him into a straitjacket and hung him off a building. He escaped."

"So how did he die?"

"He said he could take any blow above the waist and survive. So someone punched him repeatedly in the stomach till his appendix ruptured."

"And the lesson from all that?"

"No idea. But if you get to Wilkes-Barre, check it out."

Chapter 14

It's Not A Threat, It's Reality

David had been going to New York once or twice a year ever since he joined Carson. While the company's headquarters were in Philadelphia, much of its main business was conducted at its offices in New York, which occupied five floors of a thirty-story building on 56th street, between Fifth and Sixth Avenues. Linda spent at least two days a week there. The company provided her with an apartment at the Carlyle Hotel on the Upper East Side, an example of corporate largesse initiated four CEOs before Linda, which none of them had seen fit to dispense with.

David's train pulled into Penn Station at 7:05 p.m. He had forty minutes until he was due to meet Linda. He took a cab as far as 60th and Fifth and decided to walk the rest of the way. It was a warm evening, and he always liked walking in Manhattan. It was only another sixteen blocks to the Carlyle, so he could go at a leisurely pace.

The streets were busy, and Fifth Avenue, as always, was jammed with taxis all backed up trying to get through the intersections around the Plaza and the crowds spilling out into the street from the Apple Store. Three Bentleys were parked outside the Pierre Hotel. He walked past the Knickerbocker Club, where he could see a cocktail party going on through the tall windows. The tall trees of Central Park cast a thick shade over the west side of the street.

It was good to get away from Surgitec, if only for an evening. Ever since he had returned from Paris, David's life had been narrowed down to Harleysville and his hotel room. The 6 a.m. hotel gym crowd had become far too familiar. The challenge of Surgitec was much clearer in his mind, but he was still searching for the right way to go about implementing the changes he thought necessary. But thinking about them endlessly had yet to yield a solution. Instead, the problems were becoming stale, and so was his thinking. Maybe it would be easiest to just let the corporation rumble on as before. He would hardly be the first Carson executive to go this route, to just lie back and enjoy the ride without trying anything too dramatic. Wasn't that the privilege of higher echelon corporate life? Once you got to a certain level, you could only fail upward.

He crossed Fifth Avenue at 76th Street and walked staring up at the brick and limestone townhouses. There were lights on in only a few of them. Thirty million dollars a house, thought David, and their owners barely lived in them. He was looking forward to buying a home in Philadelphia and settling down after so many years on the road. He could envision the kitchen, Maria on the phone, the kids doing their homework, him coming in from work, walking over to the refrigerator and getting a beer. The life a previous generation had taken for granted, but one denied him so far by the demands of Carson. Now it was in his grasp. We'll buy the Dutch colonial with the slate roof, he thought, just as Maria wants. And we'll finally settle down.

He came to the corner of 76th and Madison and looked across to see the awning stretching out from the Carlyle across the sidewalk. Taxis were pulling up and people getting out. He waited for the light to change then walked across. The hotel seemed to radiate warmth and an old-fashioned elegance. A Broadway singer was performing in the Café Carlyle tonight and a poster of her, buxom, leaning over a piano, was stuck to a notice board. David entered through the heavy revolving door and followed the sign left into Bemelmans Bar. It was dark inside the bar, dark enough for him to have to pause so his eyes could adjust.

"David Hewitt, meeting Linda Thomas," he told the hostess.

"Ms. Thomas isn't here yet. But would you like to sit down?" David nodded and she led him through the clusters of tables to one at the back with a view of the whole room. "What can I get you while you're waiting, Sir?"

"A beer, please. Heineken." He sat down and waited. He took a handful of wasabi peas and cashew nuts from three trays set in the middle of the table. The room was about half full, a few couples, some families, and half a dozen men in suits like him conferring over drinks. He opened his briefcase and glanced through his notes. He had asked to see Linda after the latest monthly meeting of business unit heads. After his ordeal the last time around, David had been spared any questions on Surgitec. Nonetheless, Elliot had glowered at him from across the table. Then as they left the room, asked sarcastically, "So how's that whole transformation thing working out for you?"

David had tried to ignore him, but Elliot's mistrust gnawed at David's self-confidence. The fascination of working with Ed was how much it uncovered about Surgitec's business, but his concern was that it uncovered too much. Once you saw the whole edifice ripped back to the studs, did you patch it and carry on hoping to get a few more years out of it, or authorize extensive renovations? What was Carson's appetite for turning the company around? Would he really get the support that he needed to pull this thing off?

He saw Linda enter the bar, talk to the hostess, and then wave her hand at David. Linda sat down on the other side of the banquette, which curled around a corner of the table.

"You read this?" she said, throwing down a copy of *The Wall Street Journal*. David glanced at the piece he had read earlier that day. The headline read "Private Equity Firms Lining Up Bid for Carson." Three of the largest private equity companies were plotting a take-over. It would be one of the biggest in history, a massive leveraged play. "They'll immediately want to break us up. Load us up with debt, spin off several of the business units, milk the rest for cash and sell it in three to five years."

"Have you responded?"

"Not yet. Our bankers are looking at it. Of course, several of our shareholders are interested, and the board wants to consider it seriously." She turned to the waitress, "A glass of your house Chardonnay," then back to David. "It's the price you pay for underperformance. If you don't deliver, someone is always going to stick their hand up and say they can. If I were just a shareholder, and not an employee as well, I'd take it seriously. We've been stuck at twenty dollars a share or thereabouts for three years now. Everyone's wondering where our growth is going to come from. And they're right to. Anyway, how are you? When's your family joining you?"

"This weekend."

"You found a house yet?"

"We've got some viewings set up. Maria wants to be close enough to

Germantown for the Friends school."

"Sensible choice. My kids went there. Great school. You must be looking forward to having them back."

"Yes. Very much. But I don't think I'm going to have a lot of time to spend with them, at least at first. We're in the middle of this assessment with Ed."

"And how is that going?" The waitress arrived with Linda's drink. "Cheers, by the way."

"Cheers. It's pretty interesting."

"Told you it would be."

"I've never looked at a business this way," shared David.

"Incredible isn't it? You know, small businesses look at their businesses the way Ed looks at ours every single day. They worry about the profitability of every customer relationship, about the costs of adding and supporting new products, about recovering their out-of-pocket expenses. Managers in big companies like ours are spoiled. They get to think about one narrow area of the business and assume that somehow all this activity will lead to a healthy bottom line. The problem is that when you have thousands of people doing staff work, it almost always means there isn't enough attention going to line-driven revenue. Let me ask you, how many people at Carson do you think honestly believe can impact profitability?"

"Not many," acknowledged David.

"Right. The rest are doing the jobs we give them, often very well, but they're not driving profitability. They're rewarded for compliance with corporate policies, meeting regulatory requirements, following human resources procedures, satisfying service levels, everything but profit. Wow, how did we get into this so fast?"

"You asked me about Ed."

"Of course. He got you doing his top down, bottom up routine?"

"Yes."

"Customers, SKUs, territory rationalization, or as he would say, optimization."

"Exactly."

"And where does he think he can get you?"

"Twenty-six percent ROCE in eighteen months."

"You believe him?"

"It's a big stretch."

"Why do a job otherwise? How are your people taking it?"

"Some better than others."

"It was the same when I went through this. If you do everything right, you'll get seventy percent of your managers buying in on this. Twenty percent are going to keep on saying it can't be done, even if they don't say it to your face. And ten percent are going to be flat-out troublemakers. It's not going to be by department or function; it's going to be like this across the board."

"Well, I've got a ways to go to get to seventy percent buy-in."

"It's OK. Just go get them one by one. You're running this thing now. They'll take your meetings." Linda finished her drink. "I could use another one of those, but I'd better hold off. But make it in their interest to succeed. Show them this copy of the *Journal*. If they think they're going to be better off being slapped around for cash by three private equity outfits, they need their heads examined. You tell them, one by one, that you need one hundred percent buy-in for this process. And if they don't want to be a part of it for whatever reason, that's fine. They should put their hand up now. We're a large corporation and if they're any good at all, we'll find a spot for them elsewhere."

"I should make that threat?"

"It's not a threat, David. It's a reality. I was at one of those global leader summits here in New York. A guy got up, an economist, and talked about the 'new normal,' a world of slower growth, where you can't just depend on expanding markets and GDP growth anymore. To compete, you've got to optimize your own business. We are all sitting there, the heads of half the Fortune 500, all nodding our heads like puppets. We had the technology spurt in the nineteen nineties. We've got emerging markets now, but lots of local rivals and pricing pressure. The only way forward for companies like Carson, and units like Surgitec, is to make the best of what we've got. If we're not running at full capacity, it's high time we did. Or else."

"Or else what?"

"Or else someone less benign comes in and does what the shareholders want. The shareholders don't care that Surgitec has been serving hospitals for eighty years or that it supports local charities in Philadelphia. They care about future returns. It's all about profitability, David. It was all about profitability when Surgitec was growing from two hand carts and a few boxes of wooden spatulas, and it should be about profitability now. I've been around Carson enough to know that people get nostalgic for the good ol' days, and they think we should be running some sort of community service. But you know, this business grew to be what it is because of generations of managers who focused on making money. We need to get back to that before it's too late."

"That's the source of a lot of push back we're getting. There's a lot of history and it's tough to break. Ed's warned me all along, but it's still a harsh reality."

"Of course you are getting push-back. You try and change things; you're always going to run up against people who like things the way they are. You have to argue for the change without telling everyone the way they've been doing their work for years has been sub-par."

"The data has been fascinating." David removed printouts of Alice's Paretos from the inside pocket of his jacket and passed them to Linda. She peered at them in the dim light of the bar.

"Incredible, isn't it, how little we know," remarked Linda. "Sixty-one percent of your customers adding nothing to profitability. Seems like the harder you try to increase revenue, the more it costs you. What are you going to do about it?"

"If we can cut the tail, these unprofitable customers over on the right, and take out the overhead they currently absorb, I reckon that alone will yield us at least twenty-five million in profit. We have to get these customers paying what we need them to, to cover what they cost us, or else get rid of them," said David.

"I remember when Ed gave me his speech on focusing on customer-level profitability as a way to manage. He told me something I've never forgotten. 'Companies have spent hundreds of millions of dollars to take something simple and make it complicated.' From where I'm sitting now, it seems even truer than it did when I was running a business unit of Surgitec's size. All you want to do as a manager is control the basic performance of the business you're running. How many of us can say we do that? Even something as simple as that, control the basic performance. Have you gotten to the strategic imperatives yet?"

"They're a work in progress. We're obviously committed to the corporate ROCE target, and I've gotten our VP of sales on board with the idea that every customer needs to be profitable."

"That's a good start, and as I'm sure you realize, you've got to get them right. You need them to be simple enough for everyone to understand, but tangible enough for everyone to act on," advised Linda. "In addition to the two you've identified, you'll also want to maintain your market position. If you cut the too many customers, I'll have to explain to Wall Street why one of our core businesses is in decline—they, of course, can't see the data you're seeing."

David jotted down Linda's comment in his notes. It seems his boss had just passed down their third imperative:

Strategic Imperative #3:
Maintain Current Market Position

"Look, I've got to go and see our lawyers," said Linda. "They always want to meet at eight at night."

"Thanks for your time, Linda."

"I'm supporting you on this, David. I want you to succeed, and if you hit any turbulence, I'm going to help you out. But you've got to go for this thing." Linda left her newspaper on the table and walked out. After a minute, David rose and followed her. As he left the hotel, he saw Linda sitting in the back of her black Lincoln Town Car, talking heatedly into her phone. Surgitec was just a small part of her world. David owed it to her to get it right.

The lobby of the hotel where David had spent the night was bustling by 7 a.m. with business people meeting for breakfast. David took his seat on a slippery leather banquette and glanced over the menu. However tempting the eggs looked, it would have to be the Healthy Start, yogurt, granola, and orange juice. He had a few minutes. He dialed Maria's cell.

"We're getting into Philadelphia at four thirty on Sunday afternoon. Will you pick us up?" She sounded excited.

"Of course. I can't wait to see you. What have you been doing?"

"Cramming it in. Luxembourg Gardens twice yesterday. Went out to the club the day before, the kids spent the entire afternoon swimming. The night before that, I went out with the girls to Costes."

"The trendy place on Rue Faubourg St. Honore?"

"Yes. The place you hated."

"With the dance music playing while you're trying to have a drink?"

"You liked the waitresses though."

"Yeah, OK," admitted David.

"We saw Leonardo di Caprio."

"Hard life being a movie star. Not sure he ever goes out drinking in downtown Philly."

"Anything you want me to pick up before we leave? The moving guys are arriving tomorrow. We're going to spend our last night up in Chantilly, with Eric and Susan. They're only twenty minutes from Charles de Gaulle, so we won't be in such a crazy rush."

"Good idea. Maybe get me a bottle of Armagnac. I don't think it's easy to find over here."

"How's it going with Surgitec," asked Maria.

"Hard."

"Why?"

"When you come in new at the top, you don't have much time to get it right. Everyone wants to pull you in their own direction. And they all know a lot more about the business than I do. But if you want to do anything meaningful, you have to set your own course. There's a lot of hand-holding, ego massaging —I just have to be the guy giving it, not getting it."

"Isn't this what you always wanted though?"

"I guess. Be careful what you wish for. Isn't that what they say?"

"How's your hotel?"

"Fine. Lonely. I miss your cooking. If I eat another room service meal, I think I'll be sick."

"Haven't they signed you up at some fancy country club?"

"You know I can't stand those places. Not on my own, anyway. Don't want to be that guy sitting on my own at a table."

"What about the old Carson crew?"

"They're all over the place these days. And the ones here are just busy. We're all busy. I've got stacks of things to read every night. If you ever want to know about the business of surgical implement trays…"

"Save that for when I get there."

"The realtor's all lined up for Monday. She says she's got eight houses to show you. All within a twenty-minute drive of Germantown."

"Here we go again. Another move."

"I know. But this time, we'll be here a while."

"You think? You said that about Paris. That's why we brought all those old paperbacks you refuse to throw away. When's the last time you ever read any of them?"

"I know. But they're who I am. How are the boys?"

"They're happy. They won't know what they're missing."

"Better than moving when they're teenagers."

"Exactly," said Maria.

"It's not as if we wanted to raise French kids anyway."

"Smoking and listening to bad music."

"Get them back here and fill them up with real American milk…T-bone steaks."

"Apple pie."

"Teach them to play hockey, and smash someone up against the boards."

"So they can lose all their front teeth by the time they're sixteen?"

"It's the American way," said David.

"We'll come back to Paris one day, though, won't we?"

"Yes. Definitely."

"Stay at the Georges V, maybe."

"Let's see if I can do a good job at Surgitec."

"You'd better get back to work."

"See you at the airport then. I'll be the haggard looking one."

"I'll be looking tanned and relaxed."

"I hate you."

"Course you do. See you then."

David could see his guest crossing the lobby.

"David, so good to see you." Sergio Morales, David reckoned, was about ten years older than him. He had grey hair and a salt and pepper beard, and he was dressed in a navy suit, white shirt, and green silk tie, far better than most people you saw around Surgitec. He ran the company's Latin American operations. He took the seat opposite David.

"Good to see you too, Sergio. Shall we order some coffee? I get the feeling we're going to have to fight for the waiters' attention in here." Once they had placed their orders, Sergio moved aside his plate and napkin and rested his elbows on the table.

"How do you like life back in the US, David? I'm trying to remember the last time we met?"

"Panama, last year. For the Carson regional heads meeting."

"Of course. Quite a meeting."

"You had that incredible barbecue at your house. Overlooking the canal."

"Yes. And now you're running all of Surgitec. Congratulations. How are you finding it?"

"Interesting, to say the least."

"And your family? Are they happy to be back?"

"They're just getting in this weekend, so I've had a little time to just focus on the business."

"So you have some time to yourself. You can really crack the whip!"

"You could say that. And you, how is everything in Panama?"

"We're growing. More and more global companies are coming to the country to run their Latin American operations. It's a more central location than Miami."

"From what I saw, you don't have it too bad."

"You're right. And the business is growing, so what do I have to complain about? Nothing." The waitress returned with their coffee.

"Tell me about the growth."

"Where do I start? Brazil, Argentina, Mexico, we're getting stronger everywhere. As every one of these countries becomes a stronger economy, we get stronger with them. Fortunately for me, it's a very simple story."

"You're from Argentina, right?"

"Buenos Aires."

"What's the size of the business in Argentina?

"Almost twenty-one million dollars top line in the past twelve months. A record. We're putting our marker in the ground down there. When the health market consolidates, we'll be in a perfect position to reap the benefits."

"How's the rest of the region?"

"Brazil is explosive. We're seeing more new hospitals needing more supplies and we're competing aggressively on price and service. Venezuela's difficult. It used to be a very good market for us, but with so much nationalization going on and anti-American sentiment, it's become a lot harder. Mexico, Bolivia, Peru, Costa Rica, Guatemala, Panama, we're more than holding our own."

"That's very good to hear. You must be on a plane all the time."

"Once a week, at least. It's a lot of travel, but it takes me to interesting places. And we're seeing a whole new market grow up before our eyes."

"Do you need anything from me?"

"Your support, that's all. It can be hard sometimes being the foreign outpost. We're dealing with a lot of local issues, which you don't have dealing in the single US market. It means we have to juggle more on price, and sometimes our service costs go higher. But these are the costs of developing new markets. You must understand from your time in Europe."

"I know exactly what you mean. We'll get together properly very soon, I hope. You're flying out this afternoon?"

"Yes, just thirty-six hours, then back to the Canal."

Argentina, David jotted in his notes once their breakfast was over. Hadn't Alice told him it was a mess?

Chapter 15

First Inherited, Now Adopted

"What time is it in Tokyo?" said David.

"Six in the morning," said Ed. "But I've got a tray of cold noodles and green tea. I can see the sun rising over the Imperial Palace gardens. And I stopped after one sake last night, so give me your best shot."

"It's five in the evening and the sun is setting over Applebee's," said David. Ed laughed.

"You ever been to Japan, David?"

"A couple of times, but only on corporate trips. Never saw much beside the inside of the hotel."

"You should visit. Bring your family one day. The kids will love all the electronics and Manga, and you'll love the food. Japan may have its problems, but Tokyo's just about my favorite place on the planet. Last time I was here, I had this masseuse walk up and down my back. She hung onto these bars on the ceiling and walked up and down my spine for forty-five minutes. All quite proper, I assure you. But it was the greatest feeling. I'm trying to get on her scheduled this trip, but she's booked solid with every CEO in the country. And given the way the Japanese economy has been in recent years, you can't blame them."

"Listen, I wanted to talk to you because I'm getting worried about the speed of all this."

"Too slow?"

"No, no. The opposite. I'm throwing down a lot of challenges. And I'm still new here. Alice and Chris are doing some great work putting together the data, but I'm just wondering if there's a better way to do this."

"You mean a slower way."

"A more Carson way, perhaps. You know I want this to work, Ed, and Linda wants it to work…"

"But the confrontation's getting to you?"

"It's not even that. I'm worried that if the purpose of this whole process is to get everyone bought-in to a long-term transformation of the business, then we need to tread more gently."

"OK, David. We spoke about this at the start of the process. But it's different when the bullets start flying. I understand. What you're doing is bringing candor to an organization that's been starved of it. And candor always has a risk. Everyone says they want it, but at the end of the day it's the last thing they want, because if everyone's candid, there's going to be conflict. And people in large organizations much prefer to avoid conflict. The last thing they want to do is clash with the culture of their organization, whatever it may be. Most corporate processes go out of their way to avoid conflict, and give lots of accolades to the peacemakers. But think of this as a turn-around situation. By its nature it has to run up against the existing culture. You ever been on a diet, David?"

"Yes. Too many times to count."

"So why doesn't it take?"

"It does for a while. Then my willpower gives way."

"Right. So, for all these books and TV shows and pre-packaged meal programs, there's only one way to lose weight: eat better and exercise more. It's really that simple. It only gets complicated because we'd all prefer a shortcut. People don't want to eat nothing but fish, grains, and spinach, and go for runs. So we find ways to convince ourselves we can get thin by eating nothing but steak and eggs and doing a three-minute abs program."

"I'm worried that we'll do all this optimization and alignment and it won't get us where we need to go. You ever advise a small business, Ed?"

"Not for years."

"So, when I was at college, I did some work for a bakery in South Bend. It was an old, Irish place that made fantastic sourdough and soda bread. I'd met the owner after a football game and he said I could come and do a paper on his operations. I needed to study a real, live small business for my final thesis paper. So I spent time analyzing his operations, building this database of his transactions, and trying to figure out how he could be more efficient. I've been thinking about it a lot these past few weeks watching your process. What I did was kind of a miniature version of what you're trying here. So at the end, I presented to the baker and I told him he should run his ovens at different times, get rid of his trucks and rent instead, and use cheaper packaging. And he sat there patiently, listened to everything I said, and at the end he said 'thank you.' 'What do you think?' I asked him. He said to me, 'it's taken me thirty years to build this business. I've now got ovens, distribution, customers, and forty-three employees who depend on me. I could do what you're saying and make more money. But it wouldn't be nearly so much fun. I'm going to concentrate on making bread.'"

"It's a cute story, David."

"Cute?"

"Yes, cute. But it has nothing to do with Surgitec. Surgitec is not your business. It belongs to Carson and its shareholders. You can't meet payroll out of your own pocket. The employees of Surgitec aren't looking for you to be their benevolent Irish baker. They need you to make sure the company thrives and survives in the environment it inhabits. The corporate environment. Where returns matter."

"You're not the one that has to implement all this!"

"You, know, David, if you want to go low and slow, you need a different consultant."

"That's not what I'm saying."

"Sounds like it."

"It's not what I meant."

"I don't fight with people I'm advising about this, David. I'm not a body shop selling my time. Pick up the phone book, you can find any number of those guys. The reason Linda asked me to help you was because she thought my solution to your problem could work."

"Look, I can see the opportunities. The assessment is throwing them up faster than I can think."

"And now you're worried about seizing them. About implementation."

"Right."

"Here's the deal, David. You have a good business. It runs well. But you want it to be great. Carson and Linda need it to be great. But your guys there at Surgitec either don't know what great is, or don't want to do the hard work to get there. The problem is you're being too participative. It's fine. It's the Carson way. But it's only fine for status quo performance. If you want to change performance radically in a short space of time, it won't get you there. Your guys—Barry, Laura, Chuck, Larry—they'll try to wait you out. I can tell you right now, two of them at least will be having a beer saying to each other, 'This guy David, he won't last. He's on the career fast-track. He'll do something to make the numbers look good for as long as it takes to get promoted out of here and then we can manhandle the next guy.' They had it their way under George and they got comfortable with it. Whether you deal with me or someone else, the problem won't change. You can't have consensus management and have the kind of improvement corporate is demanding from you. Requiring consensus won't help you lead a team that doesn't want to go from point A to point Z."

David said nothing. His mind was racing as he looked outside his window at the curtain of trees, their leaves starting to turn golden brown and swaying in the wind. His mind drifted this way and that, unmoored and floating between conviction and doubt. He tapped the phone gently against his temple. Linda said get everyone on board. Ed said go ahead with those you can persuade. Ultimately, he was the one who would have to make this happen.

"Before we go any further," Ed continued. "You have to figure out if you want to take this on."

"What I like and hate about you, Ed, is you don't mince words."

"I'm not trying to be an asshole, David. But I need your full attention. Your return on capital isn't going to change by you doing nothing. And in the end, that's not my problem. It's yours. Your guys may think this process is some form of entertainment. You have to persuade them it's not. Are you ready for that?"

"I guess I needed a push. Yes. I'm ready. You can get back to your noodles."

"See you in a week, David."

The realtor stepped out of a new, black Range Rover. She was a short woman with straight brown hair and stony features. She wore a black pantsuit and heavy gold jewelry and carried an expensive-looking brown handbag. Either she was doing very well, thought David, or every dime she had went into her car and her appearance. He looked over at Maria who arched her eyebrows.

"I'm Diane," said the realtor, who kept her Blackberry to her ear while she extended her hand. "We've got a lot to see this morning. So just follow me."

It was a grey, overcast day. A fine drizzle was falling as they set off in David's rented Taurus.

"We're going along the Main Line. Ardmore, Haverford, Bryn Mawr, then out to Villanova," said Maria, looking at the sheaf of property descriptions Diane had given her. "Then one property in the center of town, near Rittenhouse Square. They say the neighborhood's been revived."

"It's where I've been staying. But I haven't had a chance to walk around much."

"I think it would be better for the kids to be out of the city, don't you?"

"Of course. Ride bikes, swim."

"What's the matter, David? Is something on your mind?"

"No, nothing."

"What is it?"

"Just Surgitec. There's a lot going on there right now."

"OK. Well give this some attention today, will you? It's our home."

"I'm sorry." Maria turned to look out at the passing streets. The rain was gathering on the window. "We'll find somewhere great. Don't worry."

"Is it serious, what's going on at Surgitec?"

"I'm trying to change things, that's all," confided David.

"Are you worried we're going to have to move again?"

"No, it's not that…"

"Because if there's the slightest doubt in your mind, we should rent. There's no point putting our money into a house we're only going to live in for six months. I'm happy to do that, David. You don't need to buy a house just because you think it'll make me happy."

"I know that."

"So what's the matter?"

"It's different being in charge. There's no one to blame."

"How many of those leadership courses have you gone on at Carson?"

"I know. But they're just courses. A day off from work. Actually having to do it is a completely different matter." They saw Diane pull into a driveway up ahead. The house rambled aimlessly on a perfect rectangle of green lawn. A children's play structure sat new and unused behind the house. It was one of a row of identical houses on the street. Diane stood waiting for them. David got out of the car and said "No. We told you. This is not what we're looking for."

They set off again. The next house was closer to Maria's vision. White clapboard with green shutters, and a tall hedge outside protecting it from the street. They went inside.

"This was built in nineteen thirty-two," said Diane as they walked through the living room. It had that thirties feel to it, as if Fred Astaire or Cary Grant, in their film roles as family men, lived here, went to work, and came home at six o'clock on the dot for cocktails. The wallpaper was cream, covered with tiny palm trees.

"God, I love it," said Maria as she walked through the rooms.

"This is an estate sale," said Diane. "The widow who lived here recently passed away, and her children all live in California." The kitchen had not been renovated in years, with a black and white linoleum floor and an old gas cooker. The shelves were painted apple green and were thick with dust.

"What do you think, David?" asked Maria. He was standing in the dining room looking out at the garden.

"What's that?" he said to Diane. There was a high chain-link fence twenty-five feet from the back of the house.

"The last occupant sold off an acre at the back of the property to a developer, so your garden now stops there."

David shook his head at Maria, who sighed. They got back in the car. The next two houses were a bust, one a long, skinny ranch, the other a gorgeous brick mansion that needed far too much renovation. The rain fell more heavily as the morning wore on. Diane had forgotten her umbrella and was looking ever more forlorn each time she dashed from her car to the house to fish the keys out of the lock-box. They grabbed lunch from a sandwich bar in Villanova before heading to the fifth house of the day. They pulled off the main road onto a side road that curled past a row of older stone homes, all set well back from the street.

"If she mentions curb appeal once again, I think I may have to slap her," said Maria. David laughed. They saw a few kid's bikes on the lawns in front of the houses. "This is Villanova, right? I've heard this is a great neighborhood for families." They kept driving and the houses grew larger, as did their surrounding gardens, until finally they pulled up at a rectangular stone house with leaded windows and a slate roof, glistening in the rain. Maria smiled broadly at the sight of it. David nodded.

The house smelled musty when they entered.

"Used to belong to one of the professors at the university. He left a few months ago. He wasn't sure if he'd be back, so he didn't put it on the market until last week. But as you can see, he's already moved out." There were marks on the floor and discolorations on the wall where his furniture and pictures had been. The ceilings were high and the doorways framed in dark oak. David could tell Maria was smitten.

A large, country kitchen led into a formal dining room, which in turn led out onto a stone terrace. An acre of lawn, dotted with fruit trees, stretched out behind the house and low stone walls separated their garden from the neighbors. Upstairs, the master bedroom looked out onto the garden. The bathroom fixtures were all decades old, chrome faucets and ceramic sinks, but they all worked well. There were four other smaller bedrooms set around a central staircase.

When they came back down to the living room, David took Maria's hand.

"So, do you want it?"

"Can we afford it?"

"Yes."

"Are you ready for all this, David? Really ready? Was it worth coming back from Paris for?"

"Who needs Paris?" He turned to Diane, who for the first time that day had put her Blackberry away in her bag. "Can we talk about the price?"

She pulled a file out of her bag, grabbed her calculator, and started rattling off her negotiating plan. As David scratched his signature on the offer letter, he also signed away his indecision on making the changes at Surgitec. He was digging in, and all the challenges he had inherited, he had now adopted.

Chapter 16

Put A Price Tag On Excitement

"You were in corporate strategy at Carson, weren't you?" David asked Chris. They were the first to arrive in the meeting room for the product review meeting.

"Yes. They sent me over here to get some operating experience."

"Must seem like Siberia." Chris smiled, ruefully. "How are you liking it?"

"It's certainly an experience."

"A good one, I hope. You were at Purdue, right?"

"Engineering and business major."

"Why did you choose Carson?"

"I have an uncle at General Electric. He's been there twenty-eight years. I knew I wanted to do a rotational program at a big corporation and he recommended Carson."

"Not GE?"

"I applied there."

"Didn't take you?"

"No. I got accepted," said Chris, "but I preferred the people at Carson. I'm from Scranton, so I was biased in favor of a Pennsylvania company. Didn't you do the rotational program?"

"Yes. It's a great way to learn. The only thing to bear in mind is to keep learning. And unlearning if you have to," advised David.

"People keep telling me to get comfortable with change."

"You think they're right?"

PRODUCT PROFITABILITY   Review the Team's Complete Presentation On-Line at www.smashing-silos.com

"I guess they must be. It's just a kind of curious idea. Change is always uncomfortable, so what they're saying is get comfortable with being uncomfortable."

David laughed. "And everyone thinks it's smooth sailing in corporate America."

"My friends on Wall Street think Carson must be a really conservative place, that I took the safe, boring route."

"You should have them meet Ed."

Larry Breen rapped on the door and came in, closely followed by Alice.

"Thanks for coming, Larry," said David, getting up to shake his hand. Laura Chan and Barry Johnson came in next, each accompanied by an analyst from their department. Bob Grieve and Ed were the last to arrive.

Once everyone was settled, David opened the meeting. "I wanted to get everyone together today to talk about our product line and our new product development process. As you know, Alice and her team have been analyzing our profitability in detail, including breaking out fully loaded profitability by product. Alice, let's start with your data." Alice went to the front of the room and put up a Pareto chart of revenue and profitability by product.

"Let's start with revenue," continued David. "The bottom sixty-two percent

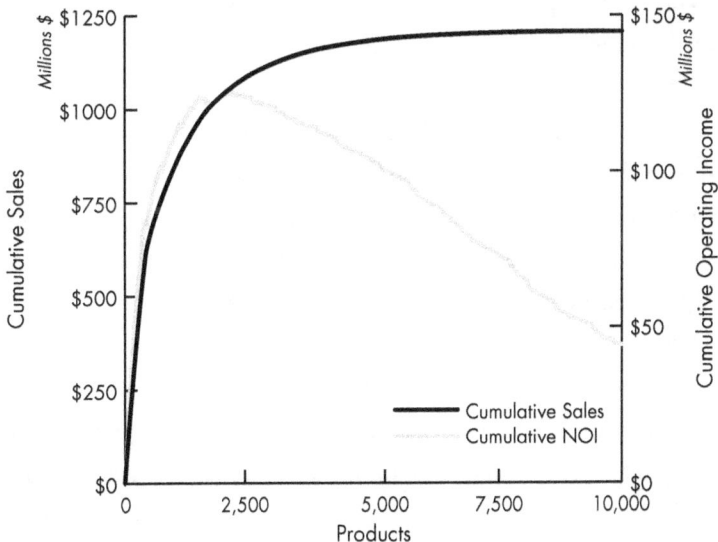

of our products produce just four percent of our sales. Four percent! And yet we know they're soaking up just as much marketing, brand management, R&D, sales, and other operating expenses as the thirty-eight percent of products that produce ninety-six percent of our revenue. It may sound cliché, but it's the same eighty-twenty rule that we're seeing in our customer base. Eighty percent of them are responsible for just a fraction of our top line, but they demand just as much service and overhead."

"We've always taken pride in the completeness of our product line," explained Laura. "Sometimes you need have some lower volume products to ensure that you can fully serve a customer's needs."

"My sales people are always clamoring for new products to pitch to customers," lobbied Barry. "It's a great reason to call, and I'll put our track of launching new lines up there with the best of 'em."

"I understand," conceded David. "I've been in both sales and marketing before, and new products are what get people excited. However, what Alice has done is put a price tag on that excitement, and sorted out just how much effort is required to support all these SKUs."

"We've been able to allocate operating expenses to specific products. We've found that all of our profits are coming from the top twenty-two percent of the products; the bottom seventy-eight percent are losing money for Surgitec," said Alice. "When we look at the performance of our new products, it's quite clear that many of our investments aren't paying off."

"Well we need to be patient with some of these products. You can't expect everything to be a hit right out of the gate," protested Larry.

"We actually looked at the profitability of all the current products by the year they were launched," replied Alice as she clicked forward in her presentation. "As you can see, the percentage of A, B, and C products is fairly constant over time. What's worse is that on average, only thirty-five percent of the products we've launched in the past five years are profitable. Plus, many of these low volume products have been in our catalog for years and years."

"I believe that the work that Alice and her team have done provides some clear direction for us on both ends of the product lifecycle: launching profitable products, and retiring unprofitable products. These are big issues to tackle, but

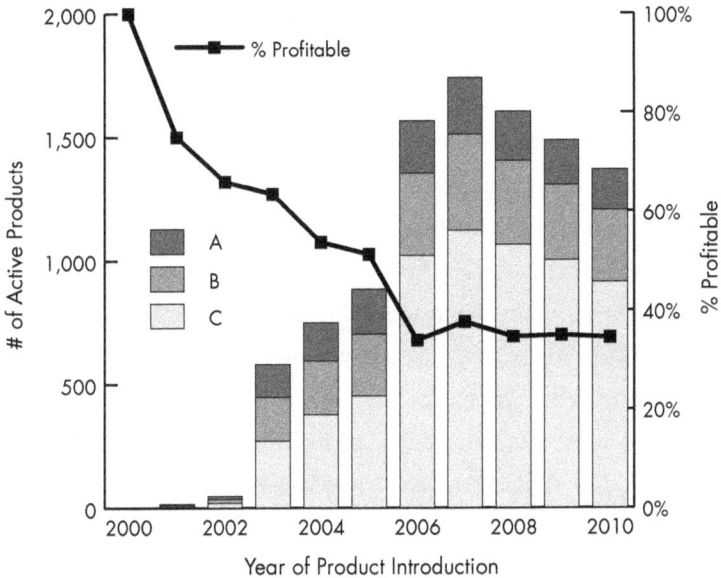

we need to do better on both counts," asserted David.

"About discontinuing products, David, understand that we have customers that are very accustomed to certain products and very loyal to Surgitec," said Barry. "We need these products to maintain our high levels of customer satisfaction."

"There are always customers who don't want to stop using your old products, and there's always customers who will want to wait for your new products before buying," interjected Ed. "It's their prerogative to make those demands, and most salespeople view it as their job to satisfy them. Add to that the need to adapt the product for individual markets, and the requests from big customers for special customizations, and you'll have just the magnitude of product proliferation that we see on Alice's chart. The way to combat those pressures is accurate profitability data, and the discipline to live by it."

"Ed's right," said David. "I'm convinced that we have an opportunity to dramatically simplify our R&D, marketing, and manufacturing work by pairing down our product line. But choosing which products to develop, and which to discontinue, aren't easy decisions. I'd like us to get this group to collaborate to make those decisions going forward, and I'd like to start the process by accessing how we've done on some recent projects. Sound good?"

As the room gave an obligatory nod, he continued. "Larry, I believe you've prepared a list of the products we've launched in the last year." Larry put up his first slide, a version of the table he had shown David on his first visit to the R&D offices, a modified GANTT chart showing the development of his recent releases. "Great. So, what I thought we could do is pick a few of these and talk through why we decided to make them, how we collaborated on their development, and how they're doing in the market. Let's start with that one, number twenty-seven on your list." David squinted to read it. "The dental mirror, DM423."

"It's one of our top sellers," said Barry immediately. "Dentists and dental surgeons love it. Gives them extra visibility into the mouth."

"I can vouch for that," said Laura. "It's really expanded our marketing beach-head in dental clinics, where we were better known for our trays, gloves, and so on."

"OK," said David. "How did we make the decision to develop this product?"

"We were getting feedback in online questionnaires that there was a new South Korean product that dentists were getting excited about," said Laura. "It was a mirror similar to ours that had this improved angle and flex in the mirror head."

"We'd done some research into this over the years," said Larry. "But we'd been making the same dental mirrors for years and there didn't seem to be a need to change them."

"My guys were hearing about this South Korean stuff on their sales calls," said Barry. "Came out of nowhere. So I told Larry we'd better get on it."

"We've been selling dental mirrors for seventy-five years," said Laura. "It's one of our core dental products, and that whole dental market is worth around one hundred and seventy million. Mirrors are maybe two to three percent of that. We hadn't changed our standard mirror for a decade or so. It was time. The South Koreans pushed us into doing what we had to do."

"We bumped up the project to the top of our R&D list, at Barry and Laura's urging. We spent two or three months on the redesign, which we then passed on to Bob and his team," added Larry.

"Bob, what's your take on this product?" asked David. Bob set down his coffee.

"This was a tricky one," he said. "We had to recalibrate to get exactly the right angle of the mirror head. That was the innovation here. And the mirror surface is made of a reflective polymer that's new for our machinery. But we got it. And the volume's been high enough to justify it. They're also very light to ship."

"Larry, did you work with Bob during the process?" asked David.

"We've been doing this a long time, David," replied Larry. "We're pretty familiar with manufacturing's capabilities."

"You comfortable with that, Bob?" Bob pursed his lips and looked off into the middle distance.

"It would have been good to have more specs earlier. Once we got the details from R&D, it was kind of a mad rush to move the mirrors into production."

"We'd already sold ten thousand of them," said Barry proudly, "just with the prototypes Larry gave us."

"We'd also put it on the cover of the catalog we send out to our dental customers," said Laura. "We had a great campaign for it. Captured all the scientific features, but still had emotion. We got some great recommendations from some of the top dental surgeons in the country saying the DM423 allowed them to see inside mouths like never before."

"So you were selling and advertising the product well before Bob had any idea how he was going to manufacture it?" said David.

"These things are never quite linear," said Barry. "We're always iterating around sales, new product development, manufacturing."

"And what happened to the older model of the mirror? Did you sunset it," asked Ed, seemingly knowing the answer in advance.

"Well, you know, a lot of the old time dentists still like that classic version. It's worth keeping around," responded Barry.

"And how many other dental mirror SKUs do you have in the line," probed Ed.

"Maybe twenty or thirty," said Laura. "As you were saying, we need to tailor them to specific markets with tweaks in packaging. Plus, if the development costs are already sunk and it's getting decent margins, why not keep selling it?"

"Actually, there are a lot of reasons to not keep selling it," said Bob. "We have to maintain tooling, materials, and QA procedures for the every product in the catalog, and train our operators and testers on their nuances. They can kill our efficiencies if we have to do a bunch of short runs."

"We also have to stock them in our distribution centers, which increases inventory, and capital employed," added Alice.

"And I guess we do struggle to bring new sales people up to speed on all these obscure SKUs," conceded Barry.

"You're all right," affirmed Ed. "and when you consider packaging, regulatory, ordering, quoting, and the people on your staffs who have to keep tabs on all this, it becomes even more costly."

"OK, I think we've covered the DM423," said David. "I like that the product concept was based on strong market demand, and that seems to explain the product's early success. But, I do think we need to get manufacturing involved earlier. It also seems we're starting to get some consensus that fewer products might actually be good for us. Whenever we launch a new product, we should have a plan in place to sunset the products it's replacing. Make sense?"

The room gave David another obligatory nod, so he continued. "Great, let's move on to the next product: the ADP-1299 Absorbent Suture."

"This is a killer product," exclaimed Larry. "One of our engineers found a new super absorbent synthetic fiber at a trade show. We were able to adapt it for use in our trauma line. We're the only supplier on the market with this new material."

The room was silent as David looked around the room for others who might share Larry's enthusiasm. "Laura, what's your take?"

"It's an interesting product. It does offer some benefits over the current standards, but unfortunately, they're not benefits that the market seems to value. We might be too far ahead of the curve on this one."

"The big issue is price," added Barry. "Our customers aren't going to pay double the market standard for a suture. This product's not selling, and our reps have figured out that it's not worth their time to try and push it."

"What's driving the price?"

"The new fiber is proprietary and expensive," said Bob. "We bought a large quantity to try and bring the price down, so now we have the added issue of sitting on all this excess inventory."

"This fiber is where the industry is headed," pleaded Larry. "We need to be patient, and be confident that we've got something unique here."

"So, we've got a unique product, but it's too expensive and not connecting with the market," paraphrased David. "Have we had success bringing these types of leading edge products to market in the past?" David looked to Laura for a response.

"We have, but we typically have a few well known doctors lined up to use and endorse the product before we launch, just like we did with the dental mirror. That gives the launch a lot more momentum. Some buzz."

"Why didn't we do that in this case?" asked David.

"We had an opportunity to do an exclusive deal with the supplier for use of their fiber in medical applications, so we had to move fast," explained Larry, his enthusiasm waning.

"Getting early adaptors is important," said Laura. "That really hurt us here."

"Plus, when we adopt a new material," added Bob, "it's best if we use it a variety of products. That improves our purchasing power and reduces our inventory risk."

"It also enables us to build a more substantial campaign around the new features, and devote more effort to sales training," added Laura.

"Yeah, my guys still really don't get why this fiber is better," confessed Barry.

"OK, I think I get it," concluded David. "The lesson here is that we need to have all the stakeholders engaged—R&D, manufacturing, marketing, and sales—and we need to have the discipline to stick to our best practices. What's next…"

"David, I want to stop here for a moment," said Ed. "What I still haven't heard in this conversation is any talk about profitability. Before you decide to pull the trigger on these new products, how do you evaluate if they're going to be profitable?"

"Well, we run all these products through our standard business development tool," said Laura.

"Tell me about that," probed David.

"With every new product, we have an evaluation tool that we use, and a worksheet that we prepare. We put in the proposed product and the one it will replace. Barry's team enters an estimate of the sales volume based on current sales and likely customers. The system matches this up with our existing contracts for similar products."

"Including all the discount and rebate programs," interrupted Barry.

"How about R&D cost?" asked David.

"No, that's separate," said Larry. "I'm not familiar with this tool. As we've discussed before, we have our budget and we try to stay within it.

"What about manufacturing?"

"Separate. Never seen the evaluation tool," said Bob.

"The tool is really designed for marketing and sales to determine if there's a realistic market for the product," said Laura. "It didn't make sense to pull manufacturing and development into it."

"What do you mean by realistic?" said David.

"It has to meet the base criteria in the tool. Then there's all the qualitative information we're getting from sales and the marketing questionnaires, which tell us what the customer is asking for."

"What are the 'base criteria'? How do you know before going into production that this product is going to be profitable?" probed Ed.

"We're looking for sales volume and gross margins that are in line with the rest of our product line," said Laura, now getting a bit defensive.

"I can see where you're going with this, guys," said Bob. "You're thinking, at what point do we put all the pieces together and think about how the new product will impact the bottom line? And you're right. We don't think about it in the development process because the assumption is that unless we're doing something crazy new, we might as well take advantage of our manufacturing, distribution and sales capacity to generate a little more revenue. Since all those costs are fixed, we might as well use the resources." The room was silent for a moment. "Isn't that what you're getting at?"

"That is exactly what I'm getting at, Bob," agreed David. "The work that Alice and her team is doing tells us that that approach isn't working for us. But I'm confident that if we have the right data and all of you are at the table when the decisions are made, we can do a much better job in making these new products a success."

"The fully-loaded profitability models we're developing aren't only scorecards for products that are in production. All the cost analysis underlying the models can also be put into worksheets to assist you in projecting profitability for new products. You'll still need to do sales estimates, but now you'll have the ability to see how those sales will flow to the bottom line," said Alice.

"But even if we do all the analysis upfront, and everyone is involved in the decision, there will still be products that don't work. That's just part of doing business," Ed continued. "However, if they're not producing within a couple years, they've got to go. Reducing the number of SKUs at Surgitec—and keeping it down—offers some real opportunities, but it will require discipline."

"It seems like we've got another strategic imperative candidate, Ed," said David as he rose to write on the whiteboard. "We've got to rationalize the number of SKUs and keep them in check going forward. Every product line and product should have financial targets, and if certain products don't meet the thresholds, they need to be retired. Everyone in the organization should know that this is a priority. How about this:"

Strategic Imperative #4:
Achieve Threshold Sales and Profitability Levels
on All Products within 3 Years of Launch

"No complaints from me," said Bob. "This will help us in manufacturing."

"It's going to be difficult for us to wean customers off of some of the older products," cautioned Barry.

"And we need some of their SKUs for international markets," added Laura.

"There's some proven tactics that we can use with your teams," responded Ed. "The most important is a substitution matrix to help salespeople find the appropriate replacement product, and to help them articulate the benefits to the customer. We'll also have to investigate ways to create universal packaging and documentation, or if that's not possible, seek local distribution partners to do that work for us."

"There's definitely some work to be done here, but it will be worth it. Now, Larry, let's keep going with your list. Number forty-three. Forgive my ignorance, but what's a sphygmomanometer?"

Chapter 17

It's The Data

"OK, what have you got for me today," asked David as he dropped into his chair in the war room. Alice, Chris, and Mike snapped to attention, sensing that David was in the mood for action. Ed closed the door so they could get to the work.

"We want to share our findings on our service delivery capabilities and our operating expenses," began Alice. "We've been using the profitability model to analyze the profitability of different customer segments and of our different distribution centers. We think we've found some definite opportunities."

"Up to this point, David, we've been focused on the Surgitec's customers and products," continued Ed. "We've found some bad deals and some dogs in the catalog, and we definitely need to fix those. But we also need to focus on getting Surgitec's cost structure to a level that it can afford with its current revenue base. We want to ensure that we can make money at prices that are competitive in the market."

"I'm with you," agreed David. "Lean and mean."

"Well, it's not just being a low cost provider," cautioned Ed. "We want to make sure the services we offer, and therefore the expenses we incur to offer them, are being rewarded by our customers. It's even true for internal functions; we need to provide support that the line units value."

"So how does the profitability model help us figure out what expenses are worth it, and which ones aren't," asked David.

"For starters, we got a lot of great insights just from the process of building

COST TO SERVE

Review the Chris and Mark's Presentation On-Line at www.smashing-silos.com

the model," said Alice. "We surveyed all the staff functions to build the allocation rules. We asked them to break down what they do, and then divide their effort by the region, product line, or customer segment that receives their services. As you've seen, once we starting using these new, more accurate allocation rules, we got a much different picture of the business."

"But that was just the start," she continued. "We took the activity break-downs that they provided us and shared it with our sales and product leaders. We asked them which of the activities were really important to running the business, and which weren't. This type of survey data will be invaluable in determining where we can cut, if we need to."

"If?" deadpanned Ed.

"Any big surprises in the survey," asked David.

"People didn't think much of international marketing," said Alice. "Twenty percent of people said it served no valuable purpose. Forty percent thought it was of low value. Only Twenty-four percent considered it critical."

"People always think that about marketing," said David. "It's always tough to measure. But try operating in this business without any brand recognition." The room didn't offer a response; they're definitely not marketing folks, thought David, but now Laura owes him one. He continued, "Any way, I take your point. There's an opportunity to trim our operating expenses without diminishing the functions we need to run the business."

"Let's dig in," prompted Ed. "Chris, you're up. Tell us about the profitability of our distribution centers." Chris stood up, walked to front of the room, and clicked to his first slide.

"Distribution costs have been consistently going up as a percentage of sales for five years," he began. "The main reason is the popularity of just-in-time delivery and inventory control systems at hospital groups. In order to cut down their storage and inventory holding costs, the hospitals are demanding more frequent deliveries and smaller loads. We've got trucks going out more often with less on them. Our distribution network just wasn't designed for that mode of operation, and we haven't been passing on the extra cost to customers."

"You have any examples," probed David.

"Definitely. There's a big hospital in Chicago that had a consulting group in last year to restructure their supply chain. Part of that was this just–in-time practice. The hospital was six months into a three year contract with us. So now we're going there four times as often as we used to with loads one quarter of the size we thought they'd be when we included delivery in the contract. Fuel costs per trip are lower because we can send a smaller truck, but labor for the driver is now four times higher."

"It's even a bigger problem when you consider the distance traveled," added Alice. "Because distribution sets delivery rates based on large, multi-state zones, we consistently lose money on the twenty percent of customers that are furthest away from our distribution centers."

"What do you recommend?"

"These hospitals are more efficient at our expense," responded Chris, returning to his original presentation. "Sales is resistant because delivery terms are stipulated in the contract, however, I think we've got more recourse than they're willing to pursue. I think we need to recoup the extra expense with delivery fees."

"And if customers refuse," asked David, curious to test the depths of Chris' work.

"It's not just about this example. There are problems like this all over the place. Distribution is treated like an afterthought to sales. And then we've got this high fixed cost of trucks and warehouses and depots, so there's not much flexibility to change our system when customers change how they want product delivered."

"What about service levels? Chuck talks a lot about this."

"Most hospitals, even the just-in-time ones, keep more than enough inventory to be able to make do if we're a few hours late, or even a few days late."

"So you think the service levels we offer aren't as critical as we think they are?"

"If you were running a hospital, would you make patients' lives dependent on the reliability of our trucking fleet? What I'm saying is that, of course, delivery is critical. Exactly when we deliver, not so much."

"We're putting too much emphasis on it then," paraphrased David.

"I'd say so," said Chris. "The cost benefit of those service levels doesn't work for us. And it gets worse the smaller the customer. When you break our customers down by segment, you can see that, however efficient our distribution system is for the large hospital groups, it's killing us when we're delivering small orders to private practices."

"That's a good point, Chris. Put up your order size analysis," directed Ed.

Chris skipped ahead, and Ed continued, "According to this analysis, you need a six thousand dollar order to break even. Yet, the median order is only thirty-four hundred dollars. You've only got a fighting chance to make money on the top thirty-five percent of your orders."

"It seems we need a distribution system that's much more efficient at moving small orders," concluded David.

"Or you need a marketing, sales, and distribution strategy that eliminates them altogether," challenged Ed. "Or at least recovers your costs when they occur."

"Do you think that's realistic," asked David. "Most of these customers don't needs truckloads of supplies at a time."

"Let's look at the segments were serving," responded Ed. "That will give us a better view."

"Mike, do you want to take over," asked Alice.

Mike strutted to the front of the room and began his presentation. "The profitability model provided a view into profitability by customer and service segment that we haven't been able to get before. We were able to join the segment definition from our customer master file, and then roll up profitability by segment."

"Was the customer master in good shape," interrupted David, aware that most customer databases are woefully out of date.

"We had to do a little manual cleansing, largely by Googling the customer and ensuring they were categorized correctly, but it could have been worse," answered Mike.

"OK, so let's see what it tells us," prompted David, returning his focus to the screen. Mike clicked to his first slide.

($ Millions)	Hospital Groups	Medical Centers	Clinics	Dental Offices	Private Practices
Sales	744	392	26	31	12
Gross Profit	373	201	14	15	6
Operating Income	39	20	(8)	-	(7)
% Profitable	65.7%	53.3%	21.9%	30.5%	22.3%

"The big headline here is that hospital chains and medical centers contribute 134% of our profits. The other segments—outpatient clinics, private practices, and dental offices—lost fifteen million dollars last year. Over seventy percent of the customers in those segments were unprofitable."

David paused as he studied the data. Wasn't there supposed to be some good news at some point in this project?

"The good news is that we know where to focus," quipped Ed. Does this guy read my mind now, wondered David to himself.

"Seriously David," continued Ed, "it actually makes the decision easier when there's a clear pattern. The data suggests that Surgitec is much more profitable in serving its larger customers, the hospital chains and the medical centers. The company's sales and distribution system was designed with these customers in mind, but going direct is just an albatross in the other segments. It reinforces Chris' analysis."

"Sales and distribution expenses combine for thirty percent to forty percent of sales in the poorly performing segments, versus less than fifteen percent in medical centers and chains," added Mike. "The gross margins seem fine, it's just that it costs us way too much to call on them, and to deliver the product."

"Put up that Pareto chart you developed, Mike," prompted Ed. "That really tells the story." Mike clicked forward in his deck.

"This is a new one," commented David aloud. "What's it telling me?"

"The dark line is our cumulative operating profit, and the lighter line is our cumulative operating expense," explained Mike. "As you can see, the further you go to the right, the more costly the customers are to serve."

"Our profit is optimal with just the top third of our customers," noted Alice. "And it's really expensive for us to serve that bottom third."

"According to this analysis, we need to bring our costs way down to fix all

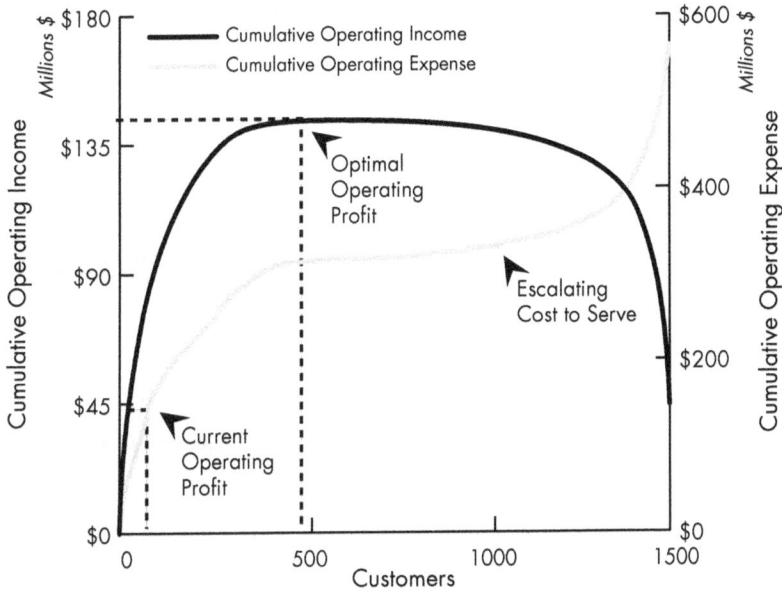

those accounts in the bottom third," observed David. "Do we have any ideas on how to get our costs down to the level were we can be profitable?"

"Actually, David, the best approach is likely to get out of that bottom third altogether, to just cut off that tail on the chart. Again, Surgitec's model just isn't aligned to that segment. You've got to call a spade a spade, and get out. Most of the work we do on costs will benefit that middle segment of customers that are mostly breakeven."

"What are your recommendations?"

"First, we could move many of these small relationships to distributors, or at a minimum send them their orders via a shipping company. It's not like these office managers aren't used to seeing the UPS guy every day," said Alice.

"Outsourcing our distribution you mean," clarified David.

"Yes, and even for many of the larger customers," responded Mike. "There are so many alternatives to us owning all these trucks and warehouses. Global supply chain companies are hugely sophisticated. They can make smaller deliveries much more economically than we can, and adapt much more quickly than we can. Customers are also be accustomed to reimbursing their vendors for those shipping costs."

"Consolidating or divesting all those expensive and underutilized distribution assets will also help us reduce our capital base," noted Alice. "Improving earnings isn't the only way to drive ROCE."

"What else," asked David.

"There's dental...," said Alice.

"What about dental?"

"Well, at least when we serve private practices and clinics, we sell them many of the same products we sell to hospitals. Dental offices are small, and require a whole specialized product line," explained Alice.

"And it's a product line that's not growing," added Chris.

"Small customers, custom products, no growth," paraphrased Ed. "It's best to exit. Even if it's break-even, it's better to reduce complexity and focus on the better opportunities."

"Sales isn't going like walking away from customers they've worked so hard to bring in, even if they are small," predicted David.

"That's true, but the data here is quite compelling. We've got two large and attractive segments that align to our service model, and three money-losing segments that don't align at all. It's clear that we need to make a change," argued Ed.

"The data *is* compelling," agreed David. "In fact, it's irrefutable. We need to restructure our approach to distribution, and get our organization thinking about the impact of our service levels on our profitability. Whether we're delivering to a just-in-time hospital customer, or a smaller clinic, we need to ensure that we can do so profitably. If it's not above our thresholds, we need to charge a fee to recover our costs." David rose from seat and strolled up to the whiteboard. "This is another area that merits a strategic imperative."

Strategic Imperative #5:
Recovery All Freight and Delivery Costs

The team nodded in agreement, and grinned with the satisfaction that their work was having such an impact.

"OK, we've got a long list of work to do here, especially when we consider potentially divesting an entire line of business," said David returning to his seat and tapping his notepad. "But it doesn't look so different from any other corporate turnaround—optimize, align, outsource, and consolidate. It's important that we communicate the depth of our approach to the rest of the company, and to the executive committee at Carson. We need to communicate what's different."

"It's the data," interjected Mike, gruffly. "It makes all the difference in the world."

"How," asked David, looking for more anecdotes to support what he already knew.

"You know how I felt about this process," Mike replied, staring hard at the table. "What changed my mind was looking at the business from the bottom up. We got away from the oatmeal of the official P&Ls. It reminded me of working for a small business, where you can actually see what costs what and where you make your money. It made me realize how little we get to see of our own company here. We're all so buried in our day-to-day work we forget what actually matters, making a good product for a healthy profit. When you get the transaction data right and build it up into customer and product P&Ls, the whole company comes into view. It's like getting the specs and instruction manual for a car when all you've been doing in the past is whacking at it with a wrench and hoping for the best."

"Do you think we can meet the ROCE target?"

"It's still going to be hard. But at least you now have an idea of how to get there. Before we had the data organized like this, I'd have given you no chance at all."

Alice and Chris nodded in agreement.

"Thank you," said David. "This has been great work. Now we need to pull this together into a presentable format and develop the business case for what these changes are worth. Make sure I have it in the next forty-eight hours. I have to persuade Carson that we're right."

Chapter 18

All Up, All In

The executive committee came to order at 9 a.m. on the dot. Linda opened the meeting.

"I realize it's hard for all of us these days with so many outside distractions. I've briefed you all individually on the progress of our talks regarding the bid being made for Carson. My position remains unchanged, that we have the resources, the vision, and the execution capabilities to continue as we are. I believe, and the board shares my view, that the shareholders and employees of Carson will be best served by retaining the current management team and ownership. A takeover would not be in the best interests of Carson. I hardly need to say, however, that we are under intense scrutiny both from investors and the media. They want to know how we intend to grow this business. It is a very fair question and one that I hope we can continue to answer vigorously and convincingly.

You will recall that several weeks ago, we asked David Hewitt to prepare a road map for Surgitec, a way to meet the ROCE target we now expect from all of our business units at Carson. He has been working on this and I believe he'd like to share his plan. David."

David could feel his breath quickening as the entire room turned to look at him.

"Thank you, Linda. And thank you all for the opportunity to conduct this review of Surgitec. I've had a chance to learn a great deal about this business and I think we're in a position now to move forward. As you all know, Surgitec

BUSINESS
CASE

Review David's Complete Business Case
On-Line at www.smashing-silos.com

has long been considered a foundation business for Carson. It occupies a special place in Carson's history, as one of its earliest and for many years one of its most profitable businesses. But in recent years, while it has continued to generate cash with minimal additional investment, it has struggled against the competition, notably lower cost rivals from Asia. Our customers have remained loyal, and our revenues have grown, but our net margins have shrunk. In this era that many are calling the 'new normal,' one of low growth and cost pressure, how is Surgitec to improve its profitability and returns on capital? Let me show you."

The door to the conference room opened, and in walked Alice, Chris, and Mike. The executives pivoted around in their chairs.

"What is this?" growled Elliot.

"This is the in-depth analysis behind what I'm about to discuss. The change that Surgitec needs." Alice, Chris, and Mike rolled out a single large sheet of paper - a business mosaic big enough to blanket a horse - made up of dozens of smaller sheets all attached with color coded tape. They taped it up along the entire length of one wall and in less than five minutes were gone.

"Since we last met, we have conducted a detailed, granular investigation of Surgitec's business. We dove all the way down to the transaction level to figure out where Surgitec makes and loses money."

"Surely not every single transaction," said Elliot.

"Every single one. Yes. From the bottom up for a full year, we rebuilt our entire P&L, allocating revenue and cost to each invoice item, and then slicing it by customers, products, channels, segments, regions, sales territories, and distribution points. Our intention is to align the different dimensions of our business: the way we price and discount, our service model, our distribution network, our product portfolio, and our customer segments. We wanted to engage all the functional areas of the business to look at how we could improve profitability."

"Didn't we do this last year," said Elliot. "George hired the very best consultants to look at exactly this."

"I've read what they produced," said David. "Their approach was more top-down. They projected a vision for the future without seeming to consider how the company works today. In order to achieve the return targets on the schedule you are demanding, it made sense to begin with the operations of the company. We tried to unpack the various discounting programs and apply them customer-by-customer. We did the same for distribution, finding that customers were being charged the same for freight regardless of how far they were from our distribution points, or in many cases not being charged at all. In R&D, we uncovered poor communication with sales and manufacturing. In short, we have found dozens of areas, small and large, where Surgitec can better align and optimize its business. But rather than me talking, I invite you to take a look. On the wall here, you will find the all data and analysis that are driving our plans. They start in the top left corner with a series of Pareto charts showing how few of our products and customers drive our net operating income. They move onto scatter diagrams, which show how our discounting practices vary widely even between customers that buy the same amount of product from us. Everywhere we looked, we found opportunities to recover lost margin."

"It looks like my kids' summer project," said Elliot, but his words were lost in the sound of the other executives rising from the table to look at the team's work. They gathered in small groups, reading, pointing and talking animatedly. Linda turned to look at David and nodded with a smile.

"So all this data came from our own sources?" asked the VP-GM of the baby-care business unit.

"Yes, all of it. We put every transaction detailed on an invoice into a data file and rebuilt it the way we wanted. The top line, gross profit, and operating profits match our financials, but the operating expenses have been completely re-allocated."

"I wish I had something like this. It's like putting on a mask and looking down into the ocean. What do you call this?"

"It's a profitability model."

"Of course. What else? Profit. The point of it all." He turned back and started talking to Linda about a chart showing the complex array of discounts offered to different customers.

"Sales must hate this," said the head of commercial finance. "You're allocating everything. There's nowhere to hide a sale made for volume alone."

"It's all up, all in," said David. "Fully loaded."

"And marketing. You're telling them that every dollar they spend on building the brand has to be assigned to a specific customer and justified against the revenue they produce for Surgitec?"

"Exactly."

"Whew."

"It's the same for everyone though. R&D has to be able to link their costs to revenue. Distribution can't just lump together extra fuel charges and dump them onto the P&L at the end of each quarter. Every dollar spent on fuel has to be charged to a customer."

"This must move a lot of customers from the black to the red and the other way round," observed one of the committee members.

"It's forcing us to look at a lot of our customers in a new light."

"You tried all this out on sales yet?" asked another.

"We've worked with them throughout the allocation process, yes."

"But you haven't told them to drop customers? Or cut volume to boost profit?"

"Not yet, but they've seen all we've been doing," answered David.

"Good luck with that," the man said, shaking his head.

"You're saying that seventy-eight percent of your small doctors' practice customers are unprofitable?" Elliot said from across the room. "If that's really true, why don't you just shut the entire business down? This can't be right."

"The problem is in distribution," said David. "These customers pay the prices we set. Where we lose out is delivering product to them using our own fleet. We'd be much better off using a third-party distributor for these customers, and having that distributor handle all the orders, deliveries, and collections. Even though we'd lose margin and a little bit of revenue in the transition, it will still be much more profitable."

"Surgitec's distribution fleet is part of Carson history," said Elliot.

"I'm aware of that. But compared to the sophistication of third-party logistics operators, our fleet is expensive and under-utilized."

Elliot flicked dismissively at another chart. "Right now, you have these unprofitable customers, according to your Excel calculations. But if you get rid of them, won't you have to spread the fixed operating costs across fewer customers?

Then you'll tip more of your customers into negative NOI. Do it again, the problem gets worse, until you have no customers and just a pile of fixed cost with no one to allocate it to."

"We're going to focus on our core segments – medical centers, hospital chains, and clinics. These segments represent ninety-six percent of revenue. Then we're going to work hard to make every customer profitable, either by increasing prices, reducing discounts, or adjusting our service levels. As for fixed cost, we're going to be aggressive in bringing the operating expenses and assets in line with the new operating plan. We'll need to consolidate some distribution centers, trim some expenses, and sell some assets. And after all, don't all costs become variable in the end?" Several of the executives laughed at the exchange.

"And this is the big one, I take it," said Linda, rapping her knuckle against one of the final sheets of paper. "The pro forma, which takes you to twenty-six percent ROCE in just a year."

(Millions $)	**Actual**		**ProForma**
Sales	1,205.9	(22.1)	1,183.8
Cost of Goods Sold	597.0	42.1	(554.9)
Gross Profit	608.9	20.0	628.9
Research & Development	104.0	34.8	69.2
Selling, General & Admin	460.6	145.0	315.6
Operating Expenses	564.6	179.8	384.8
Operating Income	44.3	199.8	244.1
Income Taxes	15.1	(67.9)	83.0
Net Income	29.2	131.9	161.1
Gross Profit %	50.5%		53.1%
R&D %	8.6%		5.8%
Operating Margin %	3.7%		20.6%
Net Margin %	2.4%		13.6%
Return on Capital %	4.5%		26.2%

"That's it," replied David. Linda took out a pair of reading glasses from her jacket pocket and peered at the chart.

"You really think you can do this? Get net operating income up to these levels?" Linda asked.

"It's all there," said David. " We boost sales by eliminating discounts for unprofitable customers and increasing prices where necessary. We transfer private practices to distribution, which reduces sales by twenty-one million dollars, but improves margins by stripping out a lot of our support infrastructure. Eliminate the fleet, as we discussed. Rationalize the product line, limit customization, streamline manufacturing. There's a lot to do. But I think there's opportunities at both ends, in terms of capturing lost gross margin and reducing our operating expenses by aligning our functions."

"What the profitability model has given us is visibility that will lead to accountability," he continued. "We can see deep into the business now in a way we couldn't before. There's no longer anywhere to hide. The levers are there for everyone to see and use to get to where we need to go. The importance of the various levers we're going to pull is illustrated over here."

Alignment Lever	Improvement Strategy	Benefit
Exit Unprofitable Segments	Exit the dental supplies business; Transfer private practices to distribution partners.	$25.7
Reduce Discounts; Optimize Pricing	Curtail discounts to unprofitable customers; Raise prices on unprofitable products.	$22.4
Optimize Product Lines	Reduce SKUs; Optimize product development process; Reduce manufacturing change-overs.	$74.0
Optimize Distribution Network	Consolidate distribution centers; Outsource portions of our fleet; Recover delivery costs.	$55.7
Streamline Sales, Support & Admin	Consolidate sales zones; Reduce overhead functions.	$21.8

"I'm impressed," said Linda, returning to her seat. At her cue, the rest of the committee sat down as well. "What are the next steps?"

"Seems like the next steps involve shutting down half the business to save money," said Elliot. Linda ignored him.

"I'd like your approval to go ahead with a new management operating system—"

"A what?" said Elliot, interrupting again.

"A management operating system."

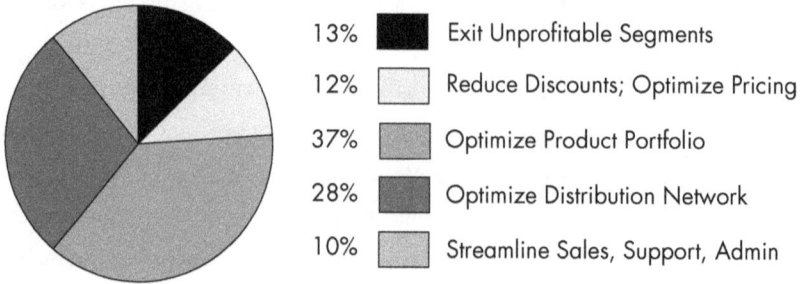

13%	Exit Unprofitable Segments
12%	Reduce Discounts; Optimize Pricing
37%	Optimize Product Portfolio
28%	Optimize Distribution Network
10%	Streamline Sales, Support, Admin

"And how does that differ from good old fashioned management?"

"It's a way of making sure everyone in the company is using the data generated by the profitability model we've built. We establish the key strategic imperatives, link them to specific financial goals, and we start to measure how we are performing against the plan."

"And how does this differ from what the rest of us unenlightened managers do?" cracked Elliott.

"Again, it's about visibility and accountability. In the past at Surgitec, we've found out we've missed our targets, but no one can tell us exactly why. A large adjustment is made to the accounts, it is charged against revenue, and we move on. What the profitability model allows us to do is establish profit goals for every single relationship. If we miss a target, we can now go down to the transaction level and piece together the reasons why. Was a customer not charged enough? Did a delivery cost too much? Was there an R&D or manufacturing expense that pushed the cost of a product too high? The individual account managers are then accountable for addressing the issue."

"It sounds terrific to me," said the executive from baby-care. "My single biggest problem is complexity. If I push here, I can't be sure what's going to happen over there. We have so many inputs and outputs to our financials, it just becomes a jumble of numbers. You hit and hope."

"Ted can say this because his ROCE at baby-care is the highest in the company," said Linda, laughing. "But now I'm wondering if he couldn't use one of these profitability models too."

"Seriously," said Ted.

"I'm not convinced," said Elliot.

"What do you propose instead," said Linda. "I think David has presented us with a very thorough analysis and proposed course of action. For me, doing nothing seems to have greater risk than David's plan."

"I think we should wait for some of the changes George implemented to kick in."

"Elliot, you know what we're dealing with beyond these walls. Inaction, I'm afraid, is not an option. David, I think you should go ahead with your plan. Let's see how you do."

Chapter 19

A Mandate, An Obligation

"We have a mandate and an obligation to transform the profitability of Surgitec," said David, standing on a platform in front of sixty senior and middle managers from across Surgitec. They were packed into a small auditorium in the basement of the company's headquarters. The air conditioning system rumbled noisily from the ceiling. "We're here today to launch an effort that will impact every department and every employee. We're asking you to change your focus, and potentially your ways, to ensure that Surgitec remains the vibrant, successful—and autonomous—company that we're all so proud to be a part of."

Rumors of David's presentation before the executive team had leaked out in advance of the meeting, and anxiety had begun to grip the company. "Over the past two years, Surgitec has achieved net operating incomes of between thirty and forty million dollars. Its return on capital employed has hovered between four and five percent. Carson, however, now expects ROCE of at least twenty percent. Going forward, our plan is to deliver twenty-six percent."

"If we wish to remain part of Carson, we have no option but to achieve this much higher return. We must grow our Net Operating Income from $44 million to $244 million." The crowd exhaled sharply. David could see Ed standing at the back of the room, one leg propped up behind him against the wall. "So how are we going to do this?"

"As many of you know, over the past few weeks, I've had a team working on a profitability model of Surgitec. The model tells us with great clarity where

STRATEGIC IMPERATIVES   Review the David's Complete Presentation On-Line at www.smashing-silos.com

we're profitable, and where we're not. The team has also collaborated with all our functional leaders—sales, R&D, marketing, manufacturing, distribution, finance, IT, and HR—to understand how our business practices impact our profitability. The purpose of this work was to achieve two things that will be vital if we are going to get to our targets: transparency and accountability."

"We need transparency so we can monitor and manage profitability at every level of the business. Transparency will enable us to make better profit maximizing decisions day in and day out. Already, we've come a long away in achieving this new level of transparency."

"Accountability means all of us will be held responsible for our financial results. All of us will be measured according to the plans we are going to lay out, and be rewarded by the degree to which we achieve them. Today, we begin our journey toward achieving this new level of accountability."

"To align our employees toward this objective, I need your support in embracing and promoting a new set of Strategic Imperatives for our company. These five key imperatives are intended to guide your decisions on a day-to-day basis. If we internalize these imperatives, and ensure that our employees do the same, I have no doubt that we'll be successful:"

SURGITEC STRATEGIC IMPERATIVES

1. Achieve a 20% Return on Capital Employed.
2. Remedy Unprofitable Customer Relationships.
3. Maintain Our Current Market Share Position.
4. Achieve Threshold Sales and Profitability Levels on All Products within Three Years of Launch.
5. Recover All Freight and Delivery Costs.

"Let me assure you, this isn't just a one off corporate initiative," David emphasized. "It's a new way of running this business, and it will cut across all our functional boundaries. There will be no more warring silos, and no more margin leakage, because everyone will be focused on the bottom line. Every cost we incur must be looked at with fresh eyes. Consider every dollar we spend and ask yourself, is this investment going to generate a twenty-six percent return?"

"I've worked at Carson for twenty-one years. I've seen the incredible things our people are capable of doing. But I've also seen people get lost. I've seen people start to think that as long as they do what they're told, someone somewhere must be thinking about profitability. What this system does is make each of us responsible. It returns this company to you. Because whatever you may think, Surgitec and Carson are no more than the sum of the people who work for them."

The applause that followed was thin and brief.

"I'm sure I'll be meeting many of you in the coming weeks as we get this up and running. And feel free to come and see me. My door is wide open for your opinions and your concerns."

"How do you think it went?" David asked Ed, as they walked briskly up to the second floor.

"You said what had to be said. Might have laid it on a bit thick at the end. But you needed to convey the gravity of the change imperative."

"Hey, I thought you told me leaders have to lead."

"I know, and you came across like every bit the field general that you need to be," affirmed Ed with a wry grin.

"Time to take the next hill, then. Let's go get sales on board."

They turned into a conference room on the sales floor. There was room for twenty around the conference room table and every seat was taken. Barry Johnson sat at one end with a couple of his lieutenants by his side. On any other day, he would have been the center of attention, noisily regaling the room with war stories. But today he was quietly studying his notes, which were covered in highlighter marks. David took the seat at the other end and waited for someone to close the door. When no one did, he did it himself. Alice sat nervously beside him. David nodded at her.

A price dispersion slide appeared on the screen behind him. He was about to begin talking when he had an idea.

"Barry. You've been involved with this project at every step along the way. Why don't you come up here and explain this to your team." Everyone in the room turned to Barry. He got up slowly and walked toward David.

"This is based on your profitability model data," he began. David felt like saying "our data" but he held back. He knew Barry remained skeptical of the change, but he could tell he was making an effort, and for that he was grateful. "It shows the various different discount rates we offer our customers, ralative to the customer's annual purchases. Each 'x' represents a different customer."

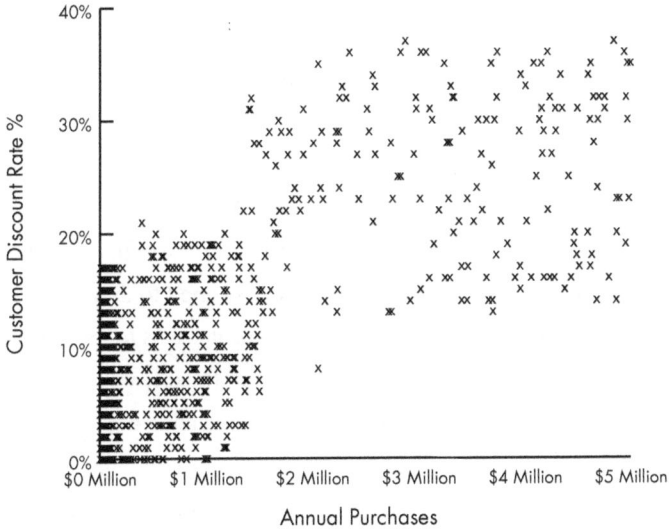

"So what does it tell us?" David asked to the room of sales leaders?

"That we're giving different discounts to different customers," said Barry. David turned to the rest of the table. He looked at a woman sitting down toward the end.

"How do you categorize your customers?" he asked her. She looked up, startled by the attention.

"Me?"

"Yes. You. It's Janet, isn't it."

"Yes." She looked pleased that David knew her name. "Well, we have various segments, and we also sell by territory…"

"I know that. But how do you categorize them? You, Janet."

"I guess, I think about our very biggest customers, the hospital chains. Then the mid-sized medical centers, and then the larger practice groups and clinics. And I guess there are the onesie, twosies, the small single practices."

"OK. How about we call them A, B, and C. This make sense to you?" Alice flashed up the chart showing profitability by customer group. "Do you want to try interpreting it?" Barry was still standing by the screen.

"That's profit along the side there?" asked Janet.

"Yes."

"Then it looks like we're doing OK with some of our A customers, a little better with our B customers and we're losing money on quite a few of our Cs."

"And why do you think that is?"

"I guess, with the As, they get a lot of discounts."

"And the Cs?"

"Cost. Are we spending too much to serve them?"

"Right. That's all there is, revenue and cost. When you're not making money, either one's too low or the other's too high. You don't need to go to Harvard Business School for that." The chill in the room seemed to thaw. "What our work has shown us is simply this: when you allocate costs to the customers who incur them, it paints a very different picture from the one we're used to seeing. The scatter chart makes one very clear point: we're giving a lot of discounts, and the discounts aren't correlated to how much they're buying, let along how profitable they are. We're even giving some big discounts to customers who are unprofitable. Right Barry?"

"If we could just eliminate discounts to unprofitable customers, our operating earnings would increase by nearly 4x - from $44 million to over $168 million just by eliminating discounts to customers who are losing us money." The room was silent.

David put up a slide making the point even clearer.

($ Millions)	Sales	Total Discounts	Average Discount Rate
Profitable Customers	860.3	(231.2)	20.4%
Unprofitable Customers	345.6	(124.4)	25.3%
All Customers	1,205.9	(345.6)	21.9%

Barry cleared his throat. "What I've committed to David, is that our team will help ensure that every customer relationship is profitable." David could not believe his ears. Barry is on-board!

"It's going to be a challenge getting them to accept changes to their discount rates. No customer wants to give up a rate they've worked hard to negotiate," said one of the zone managers from Chicago. "We think we know what they're willing to pay. But maybe with this kind of data we can make a better case."

"Tell me," asked Ed broadly to the room, "how many customers did you lose last year?"

"We're always negotiating with them," responded the Western Region VP.

"Of course. But when did you refuse a customer's price demands? And lose them as a result?"

"We take pride in always being able to work something out," said one the national account reps.

"That's probably why Surgitec has so many unprofitable customers." said Ed. "If a business doesn't lose an occasional customer on price, it's not being aggressive enough in its negotiations."

"We're only just discovering they're unprofitable with this new way of allocating costs," said Barry. "Our old methods never gave us this kind of insight."

"Exactly," said Ed. "There are costs incurred by this company to serve the customers you bring in which weren't being properly recovered. This isn't a sales problem or a manufacturing problem or a distribution problem. When a customer isn't profitable, that problem belongs to everyone. To you and everyone in this building and wherever your people work."

"Janet, which customers does it make sense to experiment with first?" asked David, stepping in before Ed got too involved with his sales force.

"I guess the smaller ones. The C's."

"What do you think, Barry?"

"If we're going to start experimenting on price, it makes sense to start small."

"So with the C customers," added Ed, "there are so many of them, you just get out the megaphone and tell them prices are going up. No point in us losing any more money selling C products to C customers. Or even B or A products for that matter."

"What about B customers," asked David.

"Don't touch them," said the VP from the West before Janet could answer. "Look at them. They're where they need to be to meet the net operating target."

"And the A's?"

"They're our biggest customers and our biggest relationships," said Barry. "We'll have to go one by one. They won't take it if we just raise prices without talking to them."

"That's fine," said David. "Makes sense. Just make sure we're rewarding them with discounts on the basis of actual orders, not promised volume that never materializes. Any discounts we offer must by earned by the customer's planned and actual behavior, not just given away because they got it last year. There's the difference. You're all going to receive training on this, and we're going to make all this data available to you. You'll be able to use the profitability model to assess the profitability of your customers. We all know what our new financial target is, a 26% return on capital employed. If a deal or a customer isn't delivering on its planned return, we should know why, and have a plan in place to fix it."

"The profitability model doesn't just give you an answer. It's not a software program where you punch in data and solution pops out. You set the target, you figure out what you need to change, and then it helps you measure the impact. The data's now so granular that you should have a much, much better view of where the problems lie. No more back of the envelope scrambles to meet your targets. You'll be able to manage your territories based on profitability data. It's simple and fit for purpose, and we can run it on our existing technology platform," said Alice.

"What's left for the salesperson to do?" said Barry.

"What do you mean?"

"If the profit target is hard and fast, it turns us into order-takers. Right now, the marketing group sets prices and we have discretion to offer discounts and rebates to close the deal. What's left for us to do," asked one of the reps.

"The sales rep has to understand the customer's budgets, and understand Surgitec's profitability, and find a deal that works for both of them. That hasn't changed, but now you've got better data and more levers to pull - including service levels, for instance - to make it happen," responded David.

"You said there are going to be objections," added Barry. "Isn't that what us sales guys love, overcoming resistance?"

"And the profit target is a minimum, right," said David. "It's not a maximum.

You can always negotiate for more." The room erupted in laughter. Even Barry could not resist a smile.

The banner hanging outside the Pennsylvania Convention Center in downtown Philadelphia read "Welcome Surgical Suppliers!" David's car pulled up at the entrance and he walked quickly up the steps and into the main hallway. A young blonde woman in a navy trouser suit approached him.

"Mr. Hewitt? I'm Jennifer with public relations."

"Thanks for meeting me here. We've got an hour, right?"

"Exactly. We've got three interviews set up, two with trade publications, the third with a local television station. They want to get your perspective on the local economy: jobs, growth, healthcare, those kinds of issues."

"Let's do it."

"Follow me then."

Jennifer walked quickly past the booths to a press tent to the left of the convention center. She directed David to stand in a corner of the tent, on an X taped to the floor. She attached a microphone to his lapel, an earpiece to his right ear, and stood back while the lights came on and the cameraman ran his checks. Three, two, one, David heard the voice of a woman reporter coming from a studio elsewhere in Philadelphia.

"We're delighted to have David Hewitt, the recently appointed President of Surgitec, one of the region's most successful and durable companies, talking to us live from Philadelphia Convention Center. David, what can we expect here in Philadelphia as the economy continues to struggle?"

"Good afternoon. And thank you for having me on your show. It's hard for me to talk for the whole city and region, but what I can say is that our business remains robust. We're launching new products, our employee base here in Pennsylvania remains solid, and we continue to grow and add new customers. So we're fundamentally optimistic about the future."

"We're hearing stories which say exactly the opposite, that Surgitec is considering a significant restructuring. Can you confirm or deny this?"

Word seems to have traveled fast, thought David. "Like every business, we are reviewing all of our operations with the purpose of improving our performance."

"Does that mean job cuts?"

"Our goal is revenue growth and improved profitability at Surgitec, and we'll do what we need to do to ensure that."

"So that's a 'yes' to job cuts, Mr Hewitt?"

"No, it's not a 'yes'. We take the livelihoods of our employees extremely seriously, and they depend on the financial health of Surgitec. As I said, we are reviewing the company and will be doing all we can to ensure that Surgitec remains vibrant and healthy over the long term."

"So maybe?"

"Your question goes to the deeper one of whether companies in the state can still compete," suggested David, hoping to change the course of the interview. "Can Surgitec remain competitive, given the challenges all American businesses face? The answer is yes, of course. But it will depend on our capacity to innovate, to respond quickly to signals from the market, and to continue serving our customers to the best of our ability. For the most part, healthcare is not something you can outsource. Surgitec and many of the other healthcare companies in this region are committed to providing the best quality healthcare for Americans and our many international customers who use our products. That remains our purpose and I think it's a pretty sustainable one. Jobs depend on growth, and I believe we're putting Surgitec on a path to growth."

"There is talk that Carson Corporation, Surgitec's parent, is an acquisition target. Does that affect you and your employees in any way?"

"I'm happy to put you in touch with Carson's spokesman to that topic, as they're in a much better position to respond to your question," deferred David. "All we can do is focus on our work and do it to the best of our ability right here in Pennsylvania, as we always have."

"Thank you, David Hewitt."

"Great job," said Jennifer as she removed the microphone and earpiece. "Let's get to your next interview."

"You think they believed me?" he asked.

"I guess we'll find out soon enough."

David had to strain to hear his buddy Jim over the noise of the crowd and the Notre Dame game playing on the television sets above the bar. "I hear you're rocking the boat over there at Surgitec, David,"

They were in an Irish pub in downtown Philadelphia. David hadn't seen Jim since Paris. David flinched as he saw a linebacker flatten Notre Dame's quarterback. "Buy me a Guinness and I'll tell you all about it."

"Are they going to be any good this season?" said Jim after ordering their drinks.

"They're always good, Jim. They're Notre Dame. The question is are they going to win many games. You always hope, but it gets harder every year. We don't get the recruits we used to." The next pass flew downfield into the outstretched hands of a wide receiver, who galloped through the secondary and into the end zone. David slammed his fist into the top of the bar. "Yessss! A little more like that." He watched the marching band go nuts, swinging their trombones round in the air and pounding their drums. Nothing like those fall afternoons in South Bend, especially when the team won. "So what are you hearing?"

"That you're shaking things up at Surgitec."

"And?"

"Not everyone's happy about it."

"What can you expect? How's biotech?"

"More talk than action."

"Still enjoying flying out to California?"

"They think we're a bunch of corporate stiffs out there, but they still want our money."

"You work with Elliot Davis, right?"

"Sure. He put me in biotech. He's been a big champion of mine," acknowledged Jim.

"For some reason, it always feels like Elliott's got it in for me."

"Probably because you're one of Linda's boys."

"No. There's something else. I don't know what it is. But it's like he's rooting for me to fail."

"No one joined Carson to take a risk, pal. We may all like to swagger round pretending we're the great business rebels, but look around. Everyone's clinging to their desks hoping for some of those big executive pay days and a comfortable retirement. What's the reward for taking a risk round here? Maybe you get a promotion. Maybe you get axed. But it's not like we're private equity guys, where you put it all out there and make $100 million for yourself."

"So you think I'm being reckless. I should just lay low."

"No. You've got to do what you've got to do, David."

"Linda's been supportive."

"Yeah, but how long is she going to be around? You read the papers. You know what's going on. If this buy-out succeeds, she's out and they'll probably bring in a CEO with a nickname like Chainsaw."

"Well, then we're all screwed. Better to do the right thing and fail than lay low and get canned anyway," said David.

"You're right," admitted Jim.

"So what are you going to do?"

"Stick it out. Wait for the right opportunity. The investment funds are getting choked off where I am and there's still not a real business there."

"You should come over and work at Surgitec."

"I'd have to be a lot more desperate to come and sell colostomy bags." David laughed so hard he almost spat out an entire mouthful of Guinness. "Look," said Jim, pointing up at the screen with one hand and patting David hard on the back with the other. "Your guys just scored again. Better hope it's an omen."

Chapter 20

Here's How It Works

"The management operating system is a process that will fundamentally transform the way you run your business," said Ed. "And now we have to implement it."

David set down the slide deck Alice had printed out for him. They were having lunch in the cafeteria at the Philadelphia Museum of Art. It was Ed's choice. They had met on the steps out front. David had spent five minutes watching one teenager after another from a school group sprint up the stairs and do the Rocky pose, arms aloft, hopping from foot to foot, gazing out over Philadelphia. If this maneuver at Surgitec actually works, he thought, he might stop by for his own victory lap.

"Here's how it works," continued Ed, snapping David's mind back into reality.

"OK, Ed. You've been eluding to the MOS for months, and I've even pitched it to the executive committee, so give me the details."

"It's your most important management tool, David. It's the technique that we'll use to translate our top-level financial objectives down to the customer and product level. It will enable your organization to act on the strategic imperatives you've established."

He pulled out a sheet of paper from his bag and drew three large circles in pencil. "There's three components of the MOS process—plans, reviews, and corrections. And they're all tied to your profitability data."

"It all begins with planning. You set the targets in collaboration with your department heads that align to the strategic imperatives. Then they have to figure

THE
MOS

Review the Management Operating System
On-Line at www.smashing-silos.com

Plan Your Accounts → Measure & Review Profitability → Take Corrective Action → (cycle)

out from the bottom up, using the profitability model, how to get there. What volumes are they going after, what prices, discounts, and fees can they set, what service levels can they afford to offer to achieve the required levels of profitability. The account plans must tie up to your overall corporate plan. It's what we've spoken about from the start, bottom up meeting top down."

"How does this differ from our current planning process," asked David.

"You've never had fully allocated profitability at the SKU and customer level before. Now, every account manager will use these metrics to plan the profitability of their territory, customer by customer. With your current process, just like many other organizations, you're focused on forecasting sales volumes, allocating quotas, setting department budgets, and committing to all the qualitative objectives that you've got as a big corporation. This is fundamentally different. You're planning profits down at the front line, and you're showing them the levers to pull to get it where it needs to be," explained Ed.

"So we're going to plan the net result, not the secondary or tertiary factors that we think contribute to it," paraphrased David.

"Exactly," agreed Ed. "Next, we're going to track our performance to that plan throughout the year. Each level of the organization will have access to the profitability model output and the variance to the plan. They'll be asked to present the results for their slice of business in management reviews each month."

"Is our profitability model data now robust enough at this stage to power the MOS? I know we're still fine tuning a lot of the allocation rules and data feeds."

"Validating the data is part of the process. If there are issues, the reps need to track them down and get them fixed. That constant scrubbing is what makes the data accurate, and what drives ownership of the issues at the front line."

"I get it. We don't want everyone just passing the buck to finance or IT. We need to make the people who manage the business—manage the customers—accountable for ensuring the data is right," agreed David.

"The final step is the most important. It's the requirement to produce specific action plans to address underperforming customers or products. This is where you're managers need to really be on point with your reps. After all, the MOS is not some sort of black box where you input data and wait for the answer. It's a process that involves prioritizing profitability, and coming up with practical tactics to improve it. By pushing P&L responsibility to the lowest levels, you're empowering those people to make the corrections."

The waitress arrived with two cheeseburgers with fries.

"God, I missed this when I was in Asia," said Ed, taking a large bite from his burger. "All that sushi makes you feel healthy, but sometimes, you need one of these."

"I had a cheese steak the other night. I could feel my arteries hardening with every bite I took."

"You ever read about the Hawthorn Effect, David," said Ed, getting back to business.

"That was a labor productivity experiment that was run back in the twenties, right?. Basically if someone's watching you, you do what you're supposed to do, even if nothing else has changed. It's kind of like the placebo effect in medicine," David replied.

"Exactly. That's the MOS. If you make people perform to the standards you set in the MOS, you'll see their behavior change immediately. They understand the plan for their piece of the business, and they know what's expected of them. If their performance falls off plan, they know they're accountable and that we're going to ask them to take corrective action. Everyone in a managerial role can now look at each customer relationship and ask 'Is this making us money?' That's the question you want asked throughout the organization."

"So that's it, huh? Seems like it's the logical conclusion for us. It will be good for the organization to get this change process behind it, and the MOS will ensure we can sustain the improved results."

"You're right about solidifying the focus, but we're far from any conclusion to this effort. You know, David, your work as a leader is really just beginning. People are going to doubt the numbers. They'll tell you customers can't cost this much to serve. That you can't raise prices. You'll have to roll up your sleeves and troubleshoot a lot of these situations. You'll have to sit with Barry and show him all his customers ranked by NOI and how you can see which are profitable and which are not. Once he sees what you're measuring and how you're linking it to his performance appraisal, he'll think twice before getting on distribution to run an express order or authorizing a change-over in manufacturing for one box of syringes."

"I'll certainly never look at overhead as just overhead again," mused David. "I don't think anyone will."

"No. Everything has to be allocated. It's curious, isn't it, how people have so many competing goals in large companies. And managers keep adding to the objectives without taking others away. Manufacturing has new union procedures, new HR policies, new safety mandates, and new quality initiatives on their plate. Then there are environmental rules, and layers of new regulation. Some people worry only about growth, while others fret about customer service. But how many focus on profitability? Wherever I go, I find these scorecard metrics that talk about procedure, volume, safety, team building, and quality, but never profit. Companies seem to forget, once they reach a certain size, that people need to drive profits. The goal of making money gets obscured by everything else. The MOS brings it back into the forefront."

Janet settled in at one of the desks reserved for visiting reps. She plugged in her laptop and opened the new file marked MOS. She had been with Surgitec for ten years, ever since graduating from college, rising quickly to her current rank as district manager for the greater Atlanta area, which included her hometown of Macon. She had always enjoyed the work—the contact with doctors and hospital managers, the quality of the products, the steady commissions. It was all so different from her sister, a realtor, who had to ride the booms and busts of her industry, with all the financial and emotional insecurity that it entailed. But this new system with its focus on profitability was something different, much different from any of the other changes that sales management had rolled out to keep everyone on their toes. Those often felt like window dressing. There was something more fundamental going on here. She took a bite of her scone and looked at a table describing her accounts.

There must be something wrong with this. She closed the file and looked for another in the email she had been sent by Barry. Nothing. This was it. She reopened it. Top of the list was HealthGroup of the South, or HGS as she often called it. It was her top account by volume and just two years ago, she had worked alongside Barry for several months toward renewing the contract. It had been a huge deal for both of them, picked out and praised at the company's annual sales conference. And now they were telling her it was unprofitable. How could it be? Every one of Surgitec's rivals would have killed for this account. She knew because she had fought them off to retain it. Meetings, dinners, negotiated discounts, charm, persistence, product demonstrations, she had rolled out the whole show to win HealthGroup of the South. If this account was unprofitable, then what was that supposed to mean for the whole company?

She glanced down the rest of her accounts, casting her mind back to the earlier meeting with David, Barry, and this consultant, Ed Chase. Her B customers looked a little better, and her small C customers seemed to be mostly losers, but the sums were trivial. She returned to HGS and started to dig deeper on the profitability data. How on earth had they screwed up the numbers this bad?

"I must confess, I was surprised," said Janet, fiddling with her pen. Across the small meeting room sat Ed and Barry. A couple of her peers sat along the perimeter of the room, waiting for their turn in the hot seat.

"Me, too," said Barry. "HGS has been a marquee account for us for many years. It's a customer with a huge halo effect. Other customers are impressed when we tell them we serve HGS. Our competitors are always fighting to lure

JANET MARLOWE (Atlanta)

Customers		Orders	Disc. Rate %	Net Sales	Net Operating Income	Annual Plan	Variance
A	Health Group of the South	456	40%	4,277,139	(583,520)	427,714	-236%
A	Plainville Medical Centers	26	32%	1,827,545	28,550	182,755	-84%
B	Atlanta Health Alliance	14	8%	975,922	347,018	97,592	256%
B	Gracewood Community Hospital	142	12%	758,739	74,210	75,874	-2%
C	Acworth Regional Medical Ctr	53	1%	299,767	55,866	29,977	86%
C	Minton Family Dentistry	3	1%	149,861	13,599	14,986	-9%
C	Vivian Wallis, M.D.	8	16%	56,755	6,110	5,676	8%
C	Rhonda-Alonso Physician Group	96	6%	54,457	(111,952)	5,446	-2156%
C	Atlanta Healthcare	17	0%	40,119	(8,014)	4,012	-300%
C	Roberta Pease, D.D.S.	13	0%	38,080	2,048	3,808	-46%
C	Thalman Trauma Center	1	3%	28,002	10,821	2,800	286%
C	Tracey-Newby Physician Group	21	12%	17,413	(25,328)	1,741	-1555%
C	Decatur Orthopedics	3	5%	7,853	(1,040)	785	-232%
C	Evans Trauma Center	3	7%	4,501	(1,818)	450	-504%
	All Customers	856	32%	8,536,155	(193,451)	853,616	-123%

them away."

"But…" said Ed.

"But, it turns out we're losing money on them," said Janet.

"How?"

"A lot of this is new to me, but it looks like our distribution costs are far higher than they need to be. It's just not something that I've ever had to pay attention to in the past. I assumed distribution had this under control."

"And did they?" said Ed.

"It's always been up to our salespeople to sell," said Barry, riding to Janet's defense. "If this was turning out to be more of a burden than we anticipated, distribution should have just told us."

"And if they had, what would you have told them?"

"Look, HGS is a huge, strategic account," said Janet.

"You know when I hear salespeople call an account strategic?" said Ed. "When they don't want to call it unprofitable. You can call HGS whatever you like, but as long as it loses money, it has no place in Surgitec's customer portfolio. That's life with our new strategic imperative."

"I'm sorry, that seems simplistic," said Janet. Barry glanced over at her with a smile. "If we just cut customers like this, we'll have no top line at all."

"So what are your options?" asked Ed. "We discussed this earlier. Now you have the data, you have to go to your customer and figure out a way to make them profitable, either by adjusting their discount or lowering the cost to serve them. Maybe both. Are you ready to have these kinds of conversation?"

"Janet has never run away from difficult situations," said Barry. "Not since she's been here and I don't think she's going to start now."

"I may need your help Barry," she said.

"You got it."

"And I've never said this before, but maybe David Hewitt's too. Trying to change things around with HGS will be quite a challenge. As sales people you're always asked to do one thing. Now you're asking a whole lot more."

"You'll have all the help you need," said Ed. "Now what about these smaller customers on your list?"

"These are our bread and butter. Small practices, clinics," said Janet.

"But many are losing money or barely breaking even," challenged Ed.

"You want me to go round one by one renegotiating them?"

"No. You need a more comprehensive strategy than that. What is it that's making them unprofitable? Is it price?"

"No. It's cost to serve," said Barry. "So having a top rep like Janet spend more time negotiating with them isn't going to be the right answer."

"So you want me to get rid of them too?" asked Janet in frustration.

"Not entirely, but we do need to think about moving them to a distributor whose costs are lower."

"This is a lot of work," said Janet. She paused briefly. "Sorry, that came out the wrong way. It's not the work I mind. It's the relationships. One of these clinics, it's a small-town clinic we just won last quarter. And now you're saying I have to go back and tell them they're going to be dealing with a distributor and not Surgitec?"

"They'll be getting the same product," said Barry, "with a service level appropriate to what they pay. It's a fair deal."

"I know, it's just…"

"I'm with you Janet. I totally understand," said Barry, leaning toward her. "You know I was a field rep and regional manager for years. These aren't numbers to you and me. They're not even just names. They're people with face and voices and feelings. And I've been thinking a lot about this myself. But if we can't make a profit serving them, we're not in business. And if we're not in business, there's no relationship anyway. So we need to figure this out, and we need you to take the lead because you're closest to them. We're not asking the moon from you or them. Just that when we do business, we're both getting a benefit. Right now, with a lot of these customers, it just isn't the case. The profitability model has given you the data. We've given you the target. I know this isn't what we've done in the past, but it's how we're doing things now."

"If you need any help digging into the data, Alice Miles can talk you through it," said Ed.

"Let's start with figuring out a plan for HGS, then work down the list," said Barry.

"OK," said Janet, closing her file. Eight million dollars a year in sales. More new customers every year for ten straight years. Job offers from Surgitec's rivals to come and work her magic for them. And now this. It felt like slap in the face.

"It comes down to just a couple of things," said Alice, sitting beside Janet at her temporary desk, "the discounts we offer HGS in our contracts and the delivery costs, which mount up since HGS places all these small orders rather than whole truckloads."

"Keep in mind it's a chain of medical facilities, not a single location," said Janet. "But when we look at this granular data, you can really see how all those orders really hurt us."

"Yes, those twenty-six different ship-tos really add up over time and we're not properly charging them for it. Look, if we break it down even more, we can see that when we ship to HGS' bigger hospitals, we're fine. But when we send our product out in small batches to its labs and satellite offices, we're getting killed. They drag down the whole account."

"I see," said Janet staring intently at the data. "So when we negotiate, we negotiate as if HGS is a single buyer. But when we serve them, we're serving them as if they were twenty-six different customers."

"That's right. They get this great deal by negotiating as a single entity, but then they behave like a series of smaller accounts," said Alice.

"So there's no real economies of scale from our side."

"Exactly. We're not charging them for service they receive. Simple as that."

"So how do we work this out?"

"We can start with each ship-to," said Alice, "and figure out what it would take to make each one of them profitable."

"OK. I get it," said Janet, typing on the keyboard. "So we set our profitability target and then figure out what it would take in terms of pricing and cost to serve to meet it for each of HGS' ship-to destinations."

"Right. And that's where you start the re-negotiation."

"So let's take this lab. We could raise the minimum order, maybe, so it covers any delivery cost. Or say you don't get the discount negotiated in the contract, unless you order this much."

"That's one way to do it. Another is to keep the existing prices the same, but

add a delivery surcharge for specific locations or orders under a certain amount."
Alice typed in some new numbers for the lab, which suddenly leapt into profit,
just below the ROCE target.

"And if we can do this for all of them…" said Janet.

"We'll hit our target. And just as important, we'll know exactly how we did
it."

"I'm impressed," said Janet, watching Alice make the numbers dance on
screen. "But can we really do this? Isn't a negotiated contract a negotiated
contract?"

"This is a three year contract, right?"

"Yes. And we're in year two."

"So it's not a long horizon," reasoned Alice.

"But for this year?"

"If this is the strategic imperative, I'm guessing you'll be need to take a go at
it. And you'll certainly have support from the top."

"I think I'll also need support from legal. But this is so helpful. I appreciate
it, Alice. It's new for me."

"I guess it'll be new for your customers, too."

"Now that, you can be sure of."

Janet stepped to the front of the room when it was her turn to present, and
clicked to her action plan for Health Group of the South.

"This is good work, Janet," said Ed, turning to her after reading the screen.

"You're learning to work this data faster than I am," said Barry.

"I had Alice to help me," she said. "She's a real pro."

"You convinced yet?" asked Ed. "Do you see when we're headed?"

"I'm impressed. I'll be convinced once I've seen how this goes down with my
customers," replied Janet.

"Fair enough," said Ed. "You spoke to legal?"

"Yes. Gave them the heads up."

"It shouldn't get that messy. Remember to tell every customer that we are
their business partner and we all need to be profitable if the relationship is to
continue. Offer to show them our costs, if you have to."

"The theory is that if we're open with our customers they'll understand our

CORRECTIVE ACTION PLAN

Account Rep:	Janet Marlowe	Date:	April 24
Account:	Health Group of the South	Zone:	South

Issues: Negative NOI; Missing Plan by $850K

Root Causes: 40% Discount Rate

Complex Network of Ship-To Locations
- Minimum Order Quantities Not Enforced
- Delivery Fees Not Assessed

Corrective Actions:

Action	Due	Benefit
1. Enforce Minimum Order Quantities	July 1	$28
2. Reduce Discount Rate to 32%	October 1	$607
3. Assess Delivery Fees for Orders Under $10,000	October 1	$92
4. Secure Orthopedic Product Sales	January 1	$130

Outcome:	Improve Run Rate to Plan	April 1	$857

argument," said Barry.

"Theories are always nice," said Janet. "Reality is often different. When I go to see HGS, we're not going to be talking theory. These are real dollars I'm going to be asking for."

"I'm with you there," said Barry. "We'll know for sure once we test this out in the field. Thanks for doing this Janet. I know it seems like a big risk to do this with your largest customer, but we need to get these numbers moving in the right direction."

"I spoke to David," said Ed. "He agreed with you. He says he'll come down to HGS. He wants to see this work more than any of us. He doesn't want you or any of the other reps feeling everything's on your shoulders. He has your back."

"It's what they call executive buy-in," said Barry, smirking.

"Call it whatever you like," said Janet. "I'll take it."

Chapter 21

Diagnosis and Treatment

David's eyes flickered open. An outdoor light filtered up through the curtains, casting shadows on the ceiling of their bedroom. He looked over at his watch. 2:47 a.m., the fourth night in a row he had woken at exactly the same time. He looked over at Maria, who was sleeping deeply beside him. As usual, his mind was racing. The workshop process had been tougher than he had thought. The process required him to get detailed agreement on all the targets that were to be loaded into the MOS. This work was tedious and exhausting, and at times bordered on being combative. Often after they had reached agreement, he had to make sure his functional leads didn't drift back to their old ways. Ed was right; it is the power of the process. It is just that the process requires a tremendous amount of work and follow-up.

David knew he wasn't going to get back to sleep. So rather than staring at the ceiling, he swung his feet down onto the floor. He walked to the bathroom and splashed water on his face. He walked down to the boys' bedroom. They were sound asleep as well. He kissed each of them on the cheek and went downstairs to his office. His computer glowed on his desk. He couldn't help himself. He began scrolling through the data from the MOS. Here and there, he could see improvement. But ROCE of 26 percent? What was he thinking?

He read the *Journal* and the *Financial Times* online, made a cup of coffee, and returned to his desk. 3:58 a.m.

Another hour before the car came to take him to the airport.

The headquarters of HGS occupied a low, glass building in an office park close to Atlanta's Hartsfield Airport.

"You ready?" said David as he and Janet entered the lobby. She nodded.

Unusually, the CEO's office was located on the ground floor, overlooking a quiet creek. As the door opened, David saw a tall man in his sixties, wearing chinos and a pale green shirt extending his hand. He looked grandfatherly and his office was covered with pictures of children and golfing trophies.

"Good morning, Mr. Manchester," said David extending his hand.

"Good morning, David," said the man in a rich, Georgia drawl. "I do appreciate you sparing the time to talk to us this morning. Coming all the way down from Philadelphia. Do call me Bo."

"Always have time for a customer, Sir."

"That's what I like to hear. Not that I ever hear it as much as I'd like these days. Do take a seat." Once they were settled and a secretary had poured everyone's coffee, Bo began to talk.

"Barry Johnson, whom I've known for years, was recently down here. We play golf together whenever we can. I used to love playing golf with your predecessor."

"George had a terrific handicap, I hear."

"You a golfer, Mr. Hewitt?"

"Nowhere close to George, I'm afraid, but I hack around."

"Well, we have some of the best courses in the world down here."

"So I've heard."

"The reason I wanted to speak to you personally, David, and I'm glad you came with Janet, was because of this pricing issue. As you probably know, we've been buying from Surgitec for over two decades. All the hospitals in our chain use your products. So, I must say, I was surprised when Janet told our purchasing folks the other day that she wanted to increase our prices. Janet has never been anything but efficient, friendly, and fair. So you can imagine, I wanted to learn where this was coming from. Get it from the horse's mouth, if you know what I mean."

"I see."

"Like I said, we've been a good customer for many years."

"I know that. But I'm sure that as a businessman yourself, you will understand our need to make a profit."

"I do understand. But these price increases seem entirely arbitrary."

"I've asked Barry to review all of our contracts, Bo, Janet's included. So please don't think we're targeting you or your company. I'm deeply grateful for your business. The issue seems to be this. Your managers are placing smaller more frequent orders, which is driving up both our manufacturing and delivery cost well beyond what we envisioned when the contract was drawn up."

"But a contract's a contract, David," said Bo.

"I understand. But I'm sure that, like me, you have a board of directors."

"I do."

"And if your profits slip, they want to know why."

"Of course."

"I'd be more than happy to share our cost analysis with you, Sir. But what it shows is that for the last two years, we've been either breaking even or losing money selling our product to you," said David.

"And a big part of this is distribution, you say?"

"Yes. Just looking at your file, you have twenty-six hospitals, clinics, and labs throughout the region, and we're making numerous small deliveries to each of them every week."

"Janet did mention this, but I wanted to hear it from you." said Bo.

"I understand. It's a big issue for you. You're as conscious of cost as we are," said David.

Bo reclined back in his chair and considered the situation. "You know, we have our own central distribution facility. We've had it up and running for two years."

"Yes?"

He paused as he thought through the issues. "We have small trucks running from there to our various hospitals all the time. I'm always trying to make sure they're properly utilized. Maybe…"

"I think I can see where you're going, Bo."

"Maybe we have you ship to our distribution hub, and perhaps a couple of the larger medical centers, and we can take care of the smaller locations," suggested Bo.

"I think that would have a big impact on our ability to keep serving you at your current discount." We can share our books with you and make sure we can all make a profit in the years to come."

"That'd be something, wouldn't it?" said Bo with a chuckle as he rose from his chair and extended his hand. "Hey, next time you come down here to Atlanta, why don't you bring your clubs?"

Janet's Camry rolled eastwards out of the city. David sat in the passenger seat reading his files.

"Is this the same way we came in from the airport?"

"No. We've got a couple of hours before you need to check in. Barry and Ed suggested I take you to see another customer."

"So they're running my schedule now?" teased David.

"I guess so."

"Who are we going to see?

"My first customer. A small, multi-doctor practice. They spend around forty-three thousand dollars a year with us. You did say you wanted to know how the 'C' customer strategy is working out."

"Is it normal for salespeople at Surgitec to take the CEO hostage?"

"I wouldn't say normal."

"Fine. You've got me now. So how is it working out with the C's?"

"Well, no one likes a change, but my customers seem to be accepting it. Now that I understand our true costs to serve these smaller locations, I understand that we need to focus on our big accounts, and let the distributors deal with these guys. I'd just hate to expose our customer base to competitors; we're really putting ourselves at risk."

"You'll be surprised, Janet. Customers are much less likely to switch vendors than most marketers or salespeople think. In most of these small practices, the buying's done by an office manager who has a certain way of doing things, and she's been doing it that way for years. The last thing she wants is to learn a new vendor's line. Plus, they know what to expect from our products. They don't want to risk getting something they might not like as much."

"So you don't think we'll lose any customers," asked Janet.

"Oh, we'll certainly lose some. But so far, it's been less than five percent of the smaller customers, and again, many of those were unprofitable," shared

David. "But tell me about the practice you're taking me to see. Have they been your customer for a long time?"

"It's actually my very first customer. I grew up around here. You know in sales, they tell you the first people you sell to are friends and family. If you can't sell to them you won't be able to sell to anyone. These guys were friends of my family."

"Is it difficult now?"

"You bet it's difficult. You've got me asking them for more money, and passing them off to a distributor."

"We simply can't afford to serve these customers directly with our current prices and cost structure. But if we can still sell to them via a distributor, who handles all the orders, deliveries and collections, maybe we can keep them. Right now, though, this channel just isn't working for Surgitec."

Janet pulled up in front of a shopping mall. The clinic was sandwiched between a gym and a mortgage broker's office. Most of the mall was taken up by a discount clothing store. The names of five doctors were listed on the sign outside.

"It's the largest family practice in Greenbriar," said Janet before they got out of the car. "But still, one of our smaller customers. How do you want me to introduce you?"

"David Hewitt from Surgitec."

"OK. Let's do it."

The waiting room was the same as doctor's waiting rooms everywhere. In the center was a coffee table piled high with old magazines. The chairs were pushed up against the beige walls. The receptionist sat behind a sliding glass window.

"Janet Marlowe for Dr. Phillips."

"You have an appointment?"

"Yes. Three p.m. We're from Surgitec."

"Ah," said the receptionist, peering gravely over the top of her reading glasses. "Please take a seat."

David and Janet sat down next to a pile of plastic children's toys. Janet picked up a year-old copy of Good Housekeeping while David glanced through some files from the office. Since his talk with Chuck, distribution had issued a request for proposals to outsource some of its operations. That was progress. After twenty minutes, a tall, thin man with think gray hair and metal-rimmed glasses appeared in the door next to reception. He wore tan slacks, a light blue shirt and stripped tie.

"Janet. Very nice to see you." Janet and David sprang out of their seats.

"Doctor, this is David Hewitt from Surgitec," said Janet.

"Hello David. Pleased to meet you," said Doctor Phillips as the two men shook hands. "Come on through to the back here so we can talk." He ushered them through to his office, a small, windowless room with gray carpeting and his various degrees hanging on the walls. A gray filing cabinet occupied one corner and a fluorescent light was attached to the ceiling. "How is your family, Janet?"

"Mom's well. Dad's still recovering from the stroke, but he's doing OK. He's moving around again."

"Happy to hear it. I hope he's watching his diet now. It was always impossible trying to tell him about it before."

"I know. He's doing his best. But I don't think he thinks life is worth living without French fries."

"And what do you do at Surgitec, David? I take it you're in sales like Janet?"

"You could say that. I'm the CEO."

"The chief executive? What are you doing in Greenbriar on a Wednesday afternoon? I'm very proud of my practice, but I'm sure we're not among your most important customers."

"All our customers are important, and Janet mentioned that you had some concerns about our new prices and distribution partners. I wanted to hear your concerns personally to ensure that I understood your perspective."

"I appreciated that, David. You know, everyone seems to think doctors are well-paid professionals. And I suppose by ordinary standards we are. But once you're done dealing with the government, insurance, and all the rest, it's not nearly as lucrative as people think. In fact, it's a struggle."

"I know."

"We've been buying from Surgitec for eight or nine years now, mainly because of Janet. But at these prices, I'm not sure we can carry on."

"We'd love to keep your business," said David. "I know it seems like a funny way of going about it. But the truth is that our distribution costs are much higher than they used to be, and we need to raise prices and restructure our delivery system to cover them."

"You know about all of these, I take it." He reached back and produced a stack of catalogs from Surgitec's rivals. "I have salesmen from these companies in here twice, three times a week. And they bring me lunch."

"If price is your only consideration, then you have a lot of choice. We understand that."

"Look, you make a good product. And I like your service. But it's not so good that I can't get it elsewhere for less. There isn't much we get to negotiate in this business. A lot of our prices are set by the government and HMOs. If I can get what I need from my suppliers at lower cost, I will."

"I fully understand your position," said David. "Let me share some of our internal records on your account. You'll see what it costs us to make and deliver product to you, and what you pay."

Dr. Phillips pulled the file over and opened it.

"What we propose is that rather buying directly from us through Janet, you place orders online with a distributor in Atlanta. They have more delivery options in this area, and you'll likely be able to consolidate your ordering with other supplies that you need. Your price will still go up, but just by a couple percent." David paused. "I hope you feel that whatever you decide, we've been honest with you."

"This is really how it breaks down for you?" asked Dr. Phillips after digesting some of the numbers.

"Yes," said David.

"So, how do you make any money?"

"In short, we make it on higher volume customers. As a percentage of sales, it simply costs us less to serve the larger customers."

Dr. Phillips looked over at Janet.

"I'm afraid we're still going to have to go with a different supplier." He closed the file. "But I'm grateful to you both for coming in. It's always good to see the diagnosis that explains the course of treatment."

Chapter 22

Me?

Bob Grieve showed David to his seat and placed a Coke in front of him.

"Thanks," said David, running a finger through the condensation on the can, and then pulling it open. "What's up?" Bob had called and asked to see him. It had been several months since David had kicked off the transformation process, and many of key changes were now in the throes of implementation.

"I'm getting a lot of push-back on the manufacturing changes."

"When we first spoke, you told me that one of the biggest problems you faced was too much complexity. R&D was throwing changes at you, sales was promising small batch orders you were struggling to fulfill. I thought you'd appreciate it when we made things simpler."

"Oh, I appreciate it. I can see what you're trying to achieve here. It makes my life a whole lot easier."

"Then what's the problem?"

"It's meant less overtime."

"I see."

"So my employees are asking for a pay rise to compensate them for the loss in overtime. If they don't get it, I'm worried about their productivity or possibly even a work stoppage."

"Boy, no good deed goes unpunished."

"I know where you stand on this, but I didn't want this coming as a surprise to you."

"No, I appreciate it, Bob." Of all his senior team, Bob had been the most helpful throughout the process. His engineering mind appreciated what David had been trying to achieve—consistency, efficiency, and the proper alignment of the company's scattershot operations.

"To them, it just feels like a pay cut," continued Bob.

"I can see that. Are we contractually committed to a certain level of O/T?"

"No, but if the worker's aren't happy, we feel it in lots of other ways. They can certainly apply pressure when they want to."

"I understand. How's it working otherwise," asked David.

"Great. Just by re-organizing our labeling process for more consistency across regions, we're saving ourselves a lot of change-overs and getting longer runs on the line."

"And you're hitting your MOS targets?"

"Easily."

"So it seems we have some latitude here," said David.

"You could say."

"If your hourly productivity has improved, based on the profitability model and MOS, then perhaps there's a way to share some of the gains with your workers."

"Incentives, you mean?"

"That's why we do anything, isn't it? In the past, their incentive was to rack up overtime hours. Now, their incentive should be efficiency and meeting higher throughput targets," said David. "If you need to change their compensation structure somehow to get them closer to where they were financially, and you can still hit your profitability targets, you should go right ahead."

"I'm a little surprised you're willing to put some money back on the table, given the targets we need to hit."

"We need to drive this mindset right down through the company, Bob. Even to the manufacturing workers. What matters is profitability. If they contribute to that, they're going to benefit."

"We're going to need to get Carson's labor relations folks involved. Our contract is tied to the corporate wide agreement, so we don't have a lot of discretion in customizing the deal," said Bob.

"Profit sharing isn't a new concept in union deals. Plus, the union is the one asking to go back to the table; we're clean on our side of the deal. We just might be able to get this done."

"Guess I better get down to corporate and see what we can do," said Bob as he stood up from his seat.

"Guess you'd better."

Chuck Long was flustered. David could tell the moment he arrived at his office. His large face was flushed and one shirttail had come untucked.

"David, do you mind if I close the door?" he said. David could hear the squeak of Chuck's thick-soled shoes on the floor. Chuck prided himself on always keeping his office door open. This must be serious. "We've just got another price hike from our major fuel supplier."

"OK."

"It's the fourth one we've had in two months. They're saying that spot prices are shooting up and they're just passing it on."

"How serious is it?"

"It's an additional ten cents per gallon, which is driving my costs through the roof. There's no way we can meet those targets in the MOS. They were set before this all happened. We're going to have to reset them."

"We're not resetting them, Chuck. It's essential that we meet the NOI and ROCE targets we have established."

"But it's impossible, when one of my single biggest costs has just gone up ten percent and I have no control. It's unfair, David."

"Have you talked to any customers about it?"

"Sales won't even discuss it."

"Let's get Barry on the phone."

"Now?"

"Right now. Dial him up." David sat back and waited for Barry's voice to crackle through the speakerphone. "Barry, it's David. I'm here with Chuck. We need to talk about distribution costs in the light of the rise in fuel prices."

"I've spoken to Chuck about this. We're talking about fixed contracts here. We've promised to deliver product at fixed prices. It's not something we can renege on. Fuel prices are always going to go up and down."

"Which is exactly why we need more flexibility around this."

"It's just not a cost we can pass on right now…"

"The fuel companies aren't squeamish about passing on the prices. If it costs more for them to supply it, they make us pay. Why shouldn't we do the same?"

"It's different," said Barry. "We made a promise to deliver at a fixed price over a certain period of time."

"If it's going to lose us money, I'm afraid it's not a promise we're going to be able to keep. You have to talk to our customers about this. It might be time to levy a surcharge to reflect the increases in our fuel costs."

"Chuck needs to run a tighter ship over there."

"Chuck's doing the best he can," said David sharply, noting Chuck's forlorn expression. "He can't control fuel prices. What we can control is how we distribute these higher costs among our customers. Our customers need us to be profitable, Barry. They know we're not running a charity. If it costs more to distribute than you budgeted for in your sales contracts, we need to re-open those contract discussions."

There was silence for a moment. Until Barry finally murmured, "I'll look into it."

"Thanks," said Chuck. "I appreciate it." The line went dead.

"You need more cost flexibility in your organization, Chuck," continued David. "If the only variable in your business is fuel prices, you need to re-think how you're set up."

"What are you suggesting?"

"You need to meet these MOS targets. It can't always be up to Barry to renegotiate with the customers, or up to me to come down here and play nursemaid to the two of you."

"Look around, David. A lot of what we do is built into the ground— warehouses, heavy trucks."

"You have to ask yourself, do you need it? Do we need all this? If fuel prices go up and you can't find any other ways to trim to meet those higher costs, you're way too rigid."

"But we've got customer service levels to meet…"

"We've talked about this. Our goal is profitability. If we're delivering a level of customer service that the customer doesn't value—a service that they're unwilling to pay a premium to receive—we shouldn't be incurring extra cost to deliver it. It's that simple. We need to talk with sales, marketing, and our customers to figure out a way to give our customers the level of service they require, and one at which we can still achieve our profitability objectives."

Chuck looked chastened. "I understand."

"Because if we don't, we may as well start putting all this great Surgitec history on the walls in boxes right now."

"I got it."

The Copa Airlines flight from New York to Panama City angled in over the Pacific Ocean. Panama City had become the preferred home for many wealthy Latin Americans, and many big corporations. The weather was good, their money was safe, and there were direct flights to everywhere in Latin America. The influx of wealth showed in the glittering line of skyscrapers along the water. David folded up his newspaper, finished his cup of coffee and prepared for the descent.

He had prepped Sergio with data from the profitability model. They had agreed on targets for the MOS, but Latin America continued to be a struggle. Much of it came down to Argentina, Sergio's home territory. The legacy office and distribution network there sucked up cash. Without it, there was a good chance the country and the region could do much better.

He looked out of the window and saw a line of container ships snaking out into the ocean, waiting to pass through the Panama Canal. Perhaps some of those containers are full of Surgitec products, thought David.

"Welcome, David," said Sergio, grasping him by the shoulder. "We have a car for you." They walked out into the blazing sunshine. The air was thick and humid. David removed his jacket and was relieved to step into the air-conditioned back seat of the black Mercedes. "You must excuse the traffic here in Panama. It is the curse of prosperity. We have more cars than we can handle, but somehow the government never has enough money to improve the roads."

Once they were moving slowly toward the city, David saw no reason to wait.

"How has this past couple of weeks been, Sergio? Are we any closer to meeting the targets we set?"

"I've set up a meeting at the office to go over the plan. But I thought we could have lunch first, at La Posta. It's a lovely restaurant with the best fish."

"But briefly, how's it working out?"

"It's working well."

"Are you hitting the targets we set in the MOS?"

"Very nearly, David. It's a work in progress."

"You see this?" He passed over a copy of the morning's Wall Street Journal. The headline on the Marketplace page read "Private Equity Funds To Continue Proxy Fight for Carson."

"They're dogged. You have to give them that."

"We have to meet the ROCE targets, Sergio. No one is exempt."

"David looked out of the window at the giant billboards advertising mobile phones. If you judged a country solely by its billboards, you'd think it was all Panamanians ever bought. It was eight months since he had joined Surgitec and five months since the MOS had been put in place. He was tired. Tired of all the objections and all the cajoling. Tired of having to be the cheerleader for this process. It was exactly as Ed had told him. It all fell on his head. For Ed, it was like pushing rope. He had to wait for someone to pull on the other end. For David, it was different. He had to force the company to follow through. He had to make them grab the rope. Was it enough to save him? Or had he been given just enough to hang himself?

Maria and the kids had settled, which was great. But he saw even less of them, he reckoned, than when they were in France. The hours were punishing. Maria was happy, but it seemed she was happy without him. His presence was almost incidental to her fixing up the house and arranging for the kids to go to school. He had become a shadow in their lives, leaving early, arriving late. His only contribution seemed to be the check that landed in their joint account every month.

La Posta occupied the ground floor of an old colonial building, painted yellow with green shutters. The maître d', an Englishman in self-imposed exile, greeted Sergio warmly. Every table in the room was taken, bar one, beside an outdoor terrace. Sergio and David were shown through to it.

"The fish here is excellent," said Sergio, when they sat down. "And they have an excellent wine selection. Would you object if I chose something?"

"Go ahead."

The waiter approached them. "A drink to start with."

To hell with it, thought David. "A glass of white wine, please."

"Pisco sour," said Sergio.

The moment they were alone again, David spoke.

"It's Argentina, Sergio. I know it's where you're from. I know it's difficult. But there's just no reason for us to be maintaining all of that infrastructure."

"I know, David."

"I don't know what else we can do to convince you. I had my team segment all your Latin American customers, the transactional versus the price buyers, the low cost to serve versus the high cost to serve, we looked at market share, share of wallet, willingness to pay, and however we cut it, it keeps coming back to Argentina."

"David, stop. I understand. I got back from Buenos Aires last night." The waiter arrived with their drinks. When he was gone Sergio began again. "My wife made me go. She reads everything you send me. She used to be a controller at a large manufacturer, so she understands all this."

"What happened?"

"She told me you were right."

"She did?"

"You know, if you go back a few years, Latin America needed a lot of help. Some of us treated American companies like guardian angels, taking their money and promising growing markets without ever delivering."

But my wife made the point that in the twenty-first century, we should not be behaving like this. She looked at the data from the profitability model and said it was time I stopped being emotional about Surgitec in Argentina and tried reason for once. You are right, David, but sometimes you need to hear it from an unexpected source."

"So what are you doing about it?"

"We've arranged with a distributor down there to take on many of the functions, the way we operate in other countries. He's going to take on most of our staff. He's expanding anyway. Of the others, two are going to take early retirement, with a very decent pension, and one already has investors lined up to open a yoga studio. She told me she'd been waiting for the right moment for years."

"What did you tell them?"

"What I just told you. That it was a moment of economic maturity. We had to do this to show our children that we can compete in the global economy without any crutches or protection."

"I'm impressed."

Sergio shrugged.

"I put it off because I was scared. I've worked with many of those people for years. I didn't want to end it. But when I did it, they understood. You forget, they read the same newspapers as us, they see the business at the ground level. They know more of what's happening than we give them credit for. When I spoke to them, you know what one of them asked me, an older woman who runs distribution there? She said, in front of everyone 'What took you so long?'"

"Thank you, Sergio. I appreciate it."

"We're still a fraction off the MOS target, but we've got account-specific plans in place to address all the variances. We'll get there, and I believe we'll get there very soon."

"That's excellent news, Sergio. I'm delighted that you and your organization are embracing the planning regimen."

"You know what changed my mind, David. About this whole process?"

"Other than your wife?"

"Besides my wife, it was two things. First was the data. I'd become far too used to playing the corporate game. I'd almost forgotten what it is that really drives this business. The second was watching you."

"Me?"

"If you'd been anything but fully committed, this would never have happened. You kept at me about this. I thought it would pass like every other corporate initiative. But you never let it go. Bob Grieve was down here recently. He sometimes comes down for the weekend if he's in Puerto Rico. We've been friends for years. And I asked him how serious you were. I trust Bob. And he said you were like a dog with a bone. You were either going to get this company turned around, or you were going to go down trying. It wasn't like that before."

"Bob's been good to me through all this."

"But enough business. You have what you want. You're in Panama now. We have wine coming. Fish. Can we please talk about something else? Anything."

David wracked his brain. All he had given his mind to these past months had been Surgitec, the data, the management operating system. It had consumed his attention. He stammered at Sergio's question. His mind was suddenly empty. Sergio looked at him pityingly.

"Don't worry David. Something will come. Cheers." David took a long sip of his wine. The ice-cold alcohol seemed to go straight to his brain. He gazed out at the sunny terrace, the blue sky above, and for the first time in months, he felt his body let go, overwhelmed by a wave of tremendous relief.

Chapter 23

They Deserve It

"You are a strange guy, Ed," said David.

"Because I ordered the onion rings again? I'm still digesting the last ones we ate here. I must be a masochist."

"You wanted to come to Applebee's. I said we could go anywhere."

"It reminds me of the old days."

"It was only sixteen months ago."

"That's what I meant. In consultant time, those are the old days."

"Anyway, it's not the onion rings," said David. "Do you remember those first few weeks? We were getting into all the dirty corners of the business. Wading through the mud."

"Happy times," mused Ed.

"It was just so depressing. Then suddenly, the moment we moved from the assessment to implementing the MOS, it was like the sun came out and you were suddenly full of optimism. It was like the sky was going to fall on our heads to anything's possible in two seconds flat."

"I could tell that you were going to make it happen, David."

"How?"

"I have a daughter," said Ed. "She's a senior in college now. But when she was in high school, she was going through a lot of changes in her junior year. She'd got a job that hadn't worked out; she had her first car, first boyfriend. And I said to her, look around at your peers. They've all been set up, like you, to succeed in life. But some will and some won't. What's going to make the difference is hunger. It's not about intellect."

"OK, so you didn't think I had any intellect," joked David.

"I once saw a TV program about this photographer," continued Ed. "And the interviewer was congratulating her on her work, and asked her 'So what's the

trick to taking a great photo?' And you know what she said? There is no trick.
There is no gift. It's about passion and hard work. I take a thousand shots to get
one. It's about hard work. You were ready to work, David. Linda saw it. I saw it."

"Thanks, Ed. I really appreciate your feedback. Would you like an update on
how the team is doing?"

"Sure. I'm anxious to hear what's everyone's up to."

"I've promoted Alice and Chris. They're now working directly for me."

"They deserve it," said Ed. "And Mike?"

"He came around in the end. But he had a real thing for manufacturing. He
left Surgitec a month ago to take a job at GE. He emailed the other day. He's very
happy."

"And the rest of them," asked Ed.

"You should see Chuck. His office looks like the Starship Enterprise. After
we outsourced most of the fleet, we invested in technology to track our deliveries
through our third-party delivery and distribution partners. He's got half a dozen
screens up there, all flickering and flashing."

"Barry?"

"Still Barry. Once we re-jigged the commission structure to reward profit not
volume, he was much more co-operative. He's still playing too much golf though."

"A company like this is always going to need a few golfers."

"Laura left. She's at P&G. Bigger budgets, more campaigns. She took several
of her people with her. I think they won some big award in their first year
over there. So marketing's now a much smaller group. Bob is still overseeing
manufacturing. We got rid of a lot of complexity and cost in his operations, but
he still has labor issues. He says it's just the way of things. R&D is still going
strong. We're funding fewer projects, but the ones that are getting budget have
the full support of sales, marketing, and manufacturing right from the start.
The engineers like knowing that their work will hit the market, rather than just
get scrapped at some point. Larry says he's getting better candidates than ever
wanting to work there. Real hotshots."

"And the ROCE?"

"Last month we got to twenty-two percent. On target for NOI of over two
hundred million dollars. We've also reduced our capital expenditures.

"Congratulations. Elliot Davis is going to love this."

"You didn't hear?"

"No. What?"

"Turned out he was passing information to the private equity consortium bidding for Carson. He thought he'd be the next CEO if the acquisition succeeded. Once Linda found out, she probably had no choice but to force him out."

"What's he doing now?"

"Sitting round the house, I think," said David. "The private equity guys dropped him like a hot rock."

"You remember how desperate all this was the last time we were here?"

"I've tried to forget it."

"Well, it was desperate. The problems seemed intractable, hard-wired into the company. And now look at you. Elliot's gone. ROCE and NOI are where they should be. You're the most upbeat guy in the world. And you know what got you there?"

"What?"

"Passion. You won this time, David. But even if you hadn't, if you kept the passion, you'd win next time. Passion will help you over any difficulty."

Chapter 24

I Told You We'd Be Back

Thwack! Jim's ball hooked left into a dense line of trees.

"How's that biotech business working out, Jim," said Marc. The four friends were back in Fontainebleau. David, Marc, Jim, and Joseph.

"Are you trying to put me off my swing?" said Jim.

"Won't make any difference. You're swinging like a dog today," jabbed Joseph.

"Go to hell."

"Seriously, what happened?"

"They don't cover Carson in Dentist's Monthly," said David. "You can't expect Marc to know."

"We got shut down, OK?" said Jim. "Carson should never have been in biotech. I'm back in paper and plastics."

"So does that mean David's now above you at Carson?"

"Look what you made me do. Can I take that shot again?"

"No!" said the three others in unison.

"Yes, David's above me, I guess, by rank."

"And salary, probably. And status," said Marc.

"And influence and likelihood to be the next CEO, or at least a division president," said Joseph.

"Do I really have to stand here and take this from a guy who makes doorknobs for a living?"

"Not just doorknobs anymore. Drawer handles, curtain rails, a complete line of fabulous home hardware."

"OK. From a guy who makes 'fabulous home hardware.'"

"When I could be making paper cups."

"The world needs paper cups."

"It needs doorknobs."

"Look, I took a risk. Didn't pan out. But life's all about taking risks."

"Sure it is," said David. "That's why we work at Carson. To take huge risks with our lives."

"Now Mr. Blue-eyed Boy here is a cynic. You turn around one bandage manufacturer and suddenly you hold the secrets to life, the universe, and everything."

"Why did you ever leave this place?" said Marc as he sent his second shot up toward the green.

"So that one day I could come back," said David.

"What's that supposed to mean?" said Jim.

"It means he didn't want to be a stooge the rest of his life," said Joseph.

"Are you calling me a stooge," complained Jim.

"Yes." Jim was the only one not laughing.

"It wasn't a sure thing," said David after they had all finished the next hole.

"So what was the secret?" said Joseph. "My business could use some of your secret sauce. Since we expanded into these new product lines, it seems like we're always chasing our tail. There's never quite enough cash, never quite enough product. The product we have isn't the right one for the market. The decorators want us to customize it, which costs more, but they don't want to pay more."

"It's about getting back to profit. You've got to use profitability planning tools to guide your everyday decisions, rather than just looking at your income statement once a month and wondering what's going on." said David

"Isn't it always about profit?" asked Marc.

"Surprisingly not. A lot of businesses put profit aside and focus purely on growth, or even just on product development," explained David. "The trick is knowing when that phase is over, and when it's time to make some money."

"I want to do both—grow and make money. What's wrong with that plan," said Joseph.

"Hey, that's everybody's plan, but it's hard. When you're entering new markets, launching new products, acquiring new customers, there are going to be lots of reasons to spend money and defer profits. You've got to be disciplined in your investments, and be willing to cut your losses if it's not working."

"Is that what was happening at Surgitec?"

"In many respects," agreed David. "Sales was excited about new customers. R&D and marketing were excited about new products. Finance and IT were excited about new systems. But Surgitec as a whole had forgotten about profitability. Fortunately, I had someone to remind me of it."

"How about you, Marc? How's your business," asked Joseph.

"I'm a dentist, not a business, Joe."

"OK. How's dentistry?"

"Very profitable, thanks."

"And what about you, Jim?" asked Joseph. "What are you going to do?"

"Following in golden boy's slipstream by the sound of it," cracked Jim.

"Seriously."

"There's worse places to be than a large US corporation," he continued. "My family is happy, if I can see it through to a soft landing, it'll have been worth it. Not spectacular. But worth it."

Maria was standing by the carousel in the Luxembourg Gardens. It was dusk, and the lights were coming on in all the grand apartment buildings around Paris. David watched his boys, now eight and five, spinning round on the wooden horses, smiling giddily.

"Chocolate," said Maria, pointing to the dark smears on their faces. "Makes every day a treat."

David took her by the waist.

"I told you we'd be back," he said.

"Thank you, Surgitec."

"We'd never really have become Parisians, would we?"

"I guess not. We're better Philadelphians."

David saw the message light appear on his phone. He had a voicemail.

"Do you mind?"

Maria shook her head. The carousel was starting to slow down. The boys screamed for another ride. David tapped in his password.

"David. Linda Thomas here. When you get back from France, we need to have a word. There's a lot of change happening here at Carson and I'd like to throw your hat in the ring—" He disconnected and tucked the phone back in his pocket. He walked back to where his sons were pleading with their mother.

For now, Carson could wait.

Acknowledgements

The amount of effort required to write *Smashing Silos* struck me as substantial at the start of the project, and became darn near overwhelming by its mid-point. Developing the fictional client environment - and all the related financial data - and integrating it into the book and the companion web site was difficult. Balancing the business lessons with an enjoyable story was the art. To assume only I performed this work would not only be inaccurate, but also almost impossible to believe. In appreciation of their impact and their assistance, please allow me to thank all those who contributed to the project.

First of all, allow me to thank and praise all the help, material and humor I have gotten from my clients over the past 30 plus years. You know who you are, and if you feel you own some part of this story, you do.

Next, allow me to sing the praises of Raja Singh, who heads up our Marketing and Sales efforts at Accunomics. From the creation of the idea through endless edits and constant manipulation of data, as well as the design of examples, Raja was clearly the most important contributor to this work. Most will never realize the amount of attention to detail and effort required in writing the book, developing the data, and creating the web site content. Raja managed all of this with great acclaim.

As you might expect, reading (and editing) *Smashing Silos* became a required activity for our team at Accunomics. Many of our consultants brought valuable perspectives to the project, and helped ensure that our story was as realistic as possible. In particular, allow me to thank my two partners, Glenn Babich and Adam Dreiblatt. It is always a great and humbling experience to have those closest to you in business provide "unfiltered" feedback on your work. I think they particularly enjoyed finding data inconsistencies and making corrections to the scenarios in the book and on the web. I look forward to returning the favor on their next project.

On the creative side, I'd like to thank Philip Delves-Broughton, a talented, creative business writer and novelist who was invaluable in structuring the manuscript and bringing the settings and characters to life in such vivid detail. Also, I thank Paige Steinman and her team at Veneer Studio in San Francisco for their great work in designing the book's cover, and for developing the interactive war room at www.smashing-silos.com.

Finally, I would like to thank my wife Francine, who endured my endless early morning trips to my downstairs office to work on my book. A consultant doesn't get to enjoy the consistent home life that many others do, so when an extra burden drives additional work during personal time, it's always a challenge. To her I owe much, but at a minimum, I need to say thanks!